WE EXPERIENCED CHRIST

CHRIST

Spiritual Encounters with Jesus Christ

Reports from the Religious-Social Institute,
Stockholm, by Gunnar Hillerdal and Berndt Gustafsson

Translated from the German by Giselher Weber

TEMPLE LODGE

Temple Lodge Publishing Ltd.
Hillside House, The Square
Forest Row, RH18 5ES

www.templelodge.com

First published in English by Temple Lodge Publishing, 2016

Originally published in Swedish under the title *He näkivät Jeesuksen* by Verbum
Förlag AB, Stockholm, 1975. Translated from the German edition, *Sie Erlebten
Christus*, Verlag die Pforte, Basel, 1979

© Gunnar Hillerdal and Berndt Gustafsson 1975
This translation © Temple Lodge Publishing 2016

A CIP catalogue record for this book is available from the British Library

ISBN 978 1 906999 86 5

Cover by Morgan Creative featuring detail of a painting by K. Martin-Kuri
Typeset by DP Photosetting, Neath, West Glamorgan
Printed and bound by 4Edge Ltd., Essex

Contents

Foreword to the English Edition

As shown in this book, most of the people reporting experiences of the risen Jesus Christ speak of 'Jesus' or simply of 'God'. The name they use may depend mainly on their religious upbringing. The authors seem to use the names 'Jesus' and 'Christ' interchangeably.

The initiate Rudolf Steiner (1861–1925) published his spiritual research about Jesus and the Christ in several series of lectures given around the year 1910.[1] In these he shows that the Christ (the Son in the Trinity of Father, Son and Holy Spirit) incarnated in the body of the human being Jesus of Nazareth for three years, from the baptism in the Jordan to the crucifixion and resurrection. This event was foretold by the ancient Hebrew prophets when they spoke of the 'Messiah'. His disciple Peter recognized Him as such when he said to Him, 'You are the Christ' (Matt. 16:16), because 'Christos', as used in the New Testament, is the Greek equivalent of 'Messiah'.

As is described in the Foreword to the German Edition, Steiner also said that the Risen One will show Himself in etheric form to more and more people after the year 1930.[2] This book reports on such events. It can give hope to persons in difficult life situations: the living Christ can be approached for help. And for those persons who had a Christ experience in our time, it may be good to know that they are not alone with their experiences.

For these reasons it is important that this book be made available in the English language, which is understood by more people around the world than any other language.

Unless otherwise indicated, Bible quotations used are from Jon Madsen's translation of the New Testament.

Monica Gold, an author published in both English and German, has helped with editing this edition. For this I thank her with all my heart.

Giselher Weber

Foreword to the German Edition

This book by Professor Berndt Gustafsson (died 1975) and Dr Gunnar Hillerdal appeared for the first time in Sweden around Christmas of 1973 (2nd edition 1979). As detailed in the Introduction, it is about a collection of reports that came into existence mainly through coincidence or a spontaneous idea. Some letters by persons who reported their unusual experiences – called with determination 'Meetings with Christ' – prompted Hillerdal, after conferring with Berndt Gustafsson, to place an advertisement into a large Swedish newspaper on 24 December 1972. The response, as Hillerdal and Gustafsson write, exceeded all expectations; the abundance and liveliness of the reports sent in was amazing.

The initiative for producing the German edition was not only the religious value of the communications, to be recognized without doubt, but also the fact that a kind of explanation – perhaps the only one that really makes sense – can be seen in a much earlier source. During the years of 1910 to 1925 Rudolf Steiner made numerous statements, according to his published works, that it would be possible to 'experience Christ in the etheric' after the year 1930 and at any rate after the middle of the twentieth century. Rudolf Steiner calls this most important happening for humanity 'The Reappearance of Christ in the Etheric'.

The indicated complex problem – on the one hand the reports of the Swedish book, completely untouched by anthroposophical viewpoints, on the other hand the statements made by Rudolf Steiner in regard to a partly parallel timeframe – has been treated by me first in the Swedish periodical *Anthropos* in June 1975, and then in a translation in the periodical *Gegenwart* (Bern, April 1976). I would like to repeat this overview here because it can contribute to placing the German edition of this book into a new, perhaps more comprehensive context.

Starting around New Year's Day of 1910 in Stockholm, Rudolf Steiner spoke very urgently about the coming revelation of Christ in our time. He said repeatedly in lectures to anthroposophists: 'First there will be a few, then more and more human beings who will see the living Christ, not in a physical but in an *etheric form.*' This would happen more and more often towards the middle of the twentieth century. The appearance of the etheric Christ would be 'the greatest mystery of the twentieth century'.

In a lecture of 25 January 1910, in Karlsruhe,[3] Rudolf Steiner says, 'The greatest, the very greatest thing can happen in the world without being noticed.' He reminds his listeners of Tacitus (*c.* AD 100 in Rome) who had very few, and wrong, ideas about the events in Palestine. This could also happen to the new revelations in our time. It is all about an appearance in the etheric world. An etheric appearance can happen simultaneously in different locations and in different forms. Christ will appear to more and more people in this sphere in the twentieth century.

On later occasions Steiner dealt with this theme in various ways and from various aspects. Astonishingly concrete descriptions exist, for instance in the Bible, of Christ as the helper, the comforter, the healer for human beings in difficulties and need. At one time Rudolf Steiner chose a wording now popular with young people:

Christ has said: 'What you have done to the least of my brothers you have done to Me.' Christ does not cease to reveal Himself to human beings, for ever and ever, until the end of the Earth. And to those who want to hear Him He says today: 'You have to look at what one of the least of your brothers thinks I think in him, and that I feel with you as you judge the other's thoughts with your own thoughts, how you are interested in what goes on in the other's soul. What you find as opinion, as a view of life in one of the least of your brothers, in that look for Me.' So speaks the Christ today into our life of thoughts, who wants to reveal Himself in a new way to the human beings of the twentieth century. We are getting close to that time . . . That is the path which today has to be called 'the Path of Thought to the Christ.'[4]

These words are amazing, for they are unusual and not easily applied to life. Nevertheless, they speak in understandable terms about the unspeakable, the innermost aspect of a truly human relationship: *The will to listen to the other, to consider what has been heard, even if one thinks it is wrong; and to throw light upon what oneself thinks is true, through the thoughts of the other.* Steiner finds this principle so important that he calls it '*the Path of Thought to Christ*'. Today, there is perhaps no better help in striving in this direction than the idea of the etheric Christ. We can fathom what this event means in today's social life with its terrible social breakups, its confusion, its deadly threats and seemingly unbridgeable differences. Christ's appearance in the etheric is the cosmic and, at the same time, the inner answer to the social enigma of our time.

Rudolf Steiner was categorical in his indications about the new revelation of Christ: 'Even if nothing is noticed, it will happen anyway.' Questions come to mind. What is the reality of this? Did anything happen? What is known about it? To demand information, to expect proof, however, is not the main idea. Because those who take hold of this don't need proof. And the others who are unable to or don't want to accept these things will, perhaps, not be convinced by the best reasons available. This happens, after all, in an intimate, subjective sphere, spiritually in the personal, and cannot be verified through outer events. On the other hand, such experiences can be passed on through the exchange of thoughts and in confidential conversations. Such communications have circulated already for some time, and many know about them. But naturally such knowledge cannot break through the barriers of small circles. For a long time it has been quiet towards the outside about such events. Now the unavoidable question arises: how can greater effects happen in the world if one always remains silent, even keeps secret, that such 'unbelievable' experiences exist that had been prophetically predicted by Rudolf Steiner? The world has a right to know about them, about what some individuals themselves have experienced, already some time ago.

Life seems to move in unexpected ways. This Swedish book has the character of a public document, without meeting any materialistic demands. It is about a number of individuals, independent of each other and not influenced by anyone or anything, who have appeared as spontaneous witnesses. One cannot bypass such a thing, regardless of any explanations and intellectual judgements. It simply is about facts. They are an unexpected confirmation of that which had been prepared by Rudolf Steiner's statements.

Boris Tullander

Preface

The decade of the 1960s was, in the view of many, a critical one for western Christianity. To a great extent the crisis was caused through a distrust of the words, the vocabulary used by the churches. However, towards the end of that decade it became noticeable that despite of this distrust the religious commitment became deeper. 'Deepening commitment' was a term used more and more, and one turned 'from the words to the reality'.

A prophetic article of 31 December 1969 in *Christian Century*, i.e. on the last day of the decade, concerned the new religious awareness as confidence in personal experience: to meet the divine directly, to experience the sacred without looking for verbal definitions or logical explanation. The path to the sacred was not opened up through contemplating problems and enigmas but through the joy and immediacy of personal divine revelation. Not the grey matter of the brain but the whole human being, all his senses — eye, ear, scent, taste, touch — were involved as organs of perception.

The material which Gunnar Hillerdal and I are presenting here shows that this deep commitment has already been present for a long time among the now living generation [1973], but is only now being recognized. A curtain has been raised and we can see now what many have seen and experienced. During the history of mysticism many have considered such experiences as described in this book 'as grace', then again 'of having been able to see Jesus'; but they are also seen as a personal secret, as a 'handshake', as a touch, concerning only that particular soul. This can explain why we know little about the occurrence of such experiences in our own generation.

As this well appeared, it did not take long to grow to an ever-increasing stream. More persons than those reporting freely of their meeting Jesus have had such experiences. Many people know such persons. In addition there are many who secretly long for such an experience. Others fear the possibility of having such an experience. And lastly, the reports available in this book are a consolation and a help for both of these groups, as far as I can see.

I also have the distinct impression that there is an increasing need to hear of reports like these. Ever since a news item on the radio on 8 January 1973 reported for the first time that people in our country [Sweden] had written to us that they had seen Jesus, a spontaneous interest in such reports grew, not least among the press. Several newspapers wanted to have the names and addresses of those who had seen Jesus. It was as if the time that had passed between the revelations of Jesus to the disciples after His resurrection and our generation had shrunk to mere days, even hours.

Names cannot be revealed here, even of those who expressly permitted it. The reports shall stand here by themselves and in the way they reached us, in some cases almost as a personal secret. Nevertheless they are personal confessions of special interest to all who ponder the reality of the Christian religion behind the words. These are testimonies but not stereotyped ones. No one had to follow a pattern, a formula of the kind one usually hears during certain services in Swedish Christendom, or of the kind I myself have proposed. The kind of reports on religious experiences shown here is new in their way of popular expression.

Questions about the genuineness of the experiences reached me quite early. There is no reason to evade such questions. Sometimes, although seldom, there were persons who were not quite clear about what they had actually experienced. But almost without exception it was about genuine religious experiences with certain characteristics: depths of feeling, a feeling that it was a 'revelation', a transformation. The experience touched the respective person at a deeper level than when for instance earlier experiences were lived through again or forgotten memories were recalled or a historic matter was imagined to be present. It is a meeting with 'the other', with reality as such. It appears as a revelation, suddenly without personal effort, unexpected. Following this, a new orientation in life and thinking, an inner and, not seldom, an outer personal transformation takes place.

Without a doubt the group of witnesses could be expanded. How many artists with a religious mission have not experienced what Simone Weil described with these words: 'When the work of art at times reaches the beauty of the sea, of the mountains, of the flowers, then it happened because the artist was filled with the light of God.' However, the testimonies reported here are enough to provide a look at religious experience in our time.

Berndt Gustafsson

Introduction: A Quite Unusual Book and its Intention

How this book came about

In 1972 the book of mine 'Who are You, Jesus?' was published (Stockholm, 3rd edition 1972), a study of Jesus interpretations today.

The first chapter of the book was entitled 'The Countenance and the Figure'. In it are reported the contradictory early Christian records concerning the appearance of Jesus. Also I stated that we have no early pictures of Jesus and that nobody knows what Jesus looked like.

After publication, I was surprised to receive letters from a few readers who thought they had seen Jesus with their own eyes. I am quoting from one of the letters:

> To have seen Jesus: A magnificent experience. But perhaps one has to be down and out in order to see Him. The sick are the ones who need the doctor. In the emptiness left by the death of my mother I believed I was unable to go on living. Prayer, intensive prayer opens the gates. A clear voice said: 'Have confidence, my daughter, your sins are forgiven.' A light attracted my eyes and I saw Jesus in a white garment standing in the garden. Around His head there were little clouds which descended gradually along the long garment to His feet. It looked like a gate. That was very beautiful ...

A great confidence and the strength to go on living—the woman went on describing in these words what this experience meant for her.

The letters I received made me think more than once. Could it be that significantly more people have unusual Christ experiences in our time than preachers and researchers imagine? Would it be possible in such a case to move persons who have experiences, something great and significant for them, to talk about it publicly?

I spoke to Professor Berndt Gustafsson of the Religious-Sociological Institute. Together we placed the following advertisement into the large newspaper *Dagens Nyheter*, Stockholm, on Christmas Eve 1972:

Tell about Jesus!

Gunnar Hillerdal says in his book 'Who Are You, Jesus?' that nobody knows what Jesus looks like. Meanwhile some readers have written and told us that they had experienced having seen Him.

We believe that many have something to tell about how they have seen Jesus or how they heard Him speak.

Write and tell us about it!

Gunnar Hillerdal, Berndt Gustafsson
Religionssociologiska Institutet,
Klara V Kyrkogata 18 A, Stockholm.

Through this ad. and the publicity which our imminent investigation received later in the press we got in contact with an astonishing number of people. Over a hundred documents about this are in the archives of the Religious-Sociological Institute.

The main chapters of this book reproduce the more important documents in an edited form. For understandable reasons, most of the writers have asked that their names not be mentioned in the publication. Of course, we have respected this wish. In a few cases, however, the names were published, namely those published previously in print or otherwise, or in cases where the authors had expressly permitted that their names be published.

The people who have written to us hail from quite a variety of occupations: a businessman, a white-collar worker of advanced rank, a nurse, somebody for whom it was important that he was a common, simple labourer, a priest of the Swedish Church — just to name a few as examples. In all cases, they turned to us in confidence in order to report their quite personal and highly valued experiences.

The aim of this book

The book has a serious aim. We are not endeavouring to sensationalize despite the fact that the research excited justified attention and that the publication certainly will create more of it.

We believe we are undertaking a task in religious-psychological science. Among other things, we can state that unusual Christ-experiences are more frequent than many researchers seem to believe. Through the ample material available to us, we have found it possible to make a distinction between visionary and auditory impressions arising from a healthy religious life and, by contrast, unhealthy, pathological elements in so-called revelations. It has been shown previously that completely normal, healthy human beings who have had an intense spiritual life can experience visionary and auditory impressions, for instance by Hjalmar Sundén (in the book 'Man and Religion'). Our material confirms this convincingly.

We believe that we are also serving the Church and its message through the research which we initiated. Quite a few reports show that persons who had experienced a living, present Christ had previously shied away from communicating their experiences, not only because they were precious to them, were of personal intimacy and are holy — of this certain documents speak clearly — but also because the prevailing cultural climate was such that they did not want to risk, through telling, to be seen as being eccentric. To refute such a view is important for the Church as well as for promoting the truth.

In addition, there is a circumstance very important to me. The documents we were allowed to publish are in many cases wonderfully human. When I read them myself I was deeply moved. I dare to believe that the publication will mean a great deal to many. The selection of documents, as published with slight editing and with a few commentaries, could become a book for devotion—not of the usual kind.

Gunnar Hillerdal

1. 'The Lord is near those who are of humble spirit'

In Psalm 34:18 we can read the words: 'The Lord is near those who are of humble and depressed spirit. He hears the sighs of those ready to atone and He turns towards their prayers.'

Jesus is the comforter. The reader experiences these light-filled words in many descriptions of the New Testament. Jesus is near those in grief and in sorrow. 'Just as the share we have in the sufferings of Christ grows constantly so the comfort of the spirit increases constantly in us through Christ,' Paul wrote in his second letter to the congregation in Corinth (2 Cor. 1:5). In the Sermon on the Mount Jesus says: 'Blessed are those who endure earthly suffering, for within themselves they find the comfort of the spirit' (Matt. 5:4).

Jesus comforted a woman during the days after the murder of President Kennedy

In Report No. 58 a woman wrote:

> It was in the days after the murder of President Kennedy. It seemed to me that all hope for the future was lost — not for me personally, but for the possibilities of the world, for mankind ...

The woman said she did not have any faith in God. She even could not remember her beliefs of her childhood.

> For all the time I was conscious of myself I did not have any faith. But neither did I deny my faith. I just found all this, to say it mildly, improbable. I was astounded that so-called enlightened persons could believe.

After the news of the murder she had a desperate need to hear something publicly about the enormous loss for the world. She went into a Roman Catholic Church because the president had been a Catholic. But she did not get an answer to what affected her. She telephoned political organizations in order to find out whether appropriate public appreciations were being planned. But also there she did not receive a satisfying answer.

> On the Saturday after the murder I visited an evening service for the first time in my life ... In his sermon the minister mentioned with a few words just what moved me so much. But especially then I was overcome with grief so deep that I cannot say how much it moved me. Tears streamed from my eyes.

She interrupted her tale by pointing out that she never had cried in public except at funerals of people close and dear to her. She continued:

> And at this moment this peculiar, inconceivable, but wonderful thing happened. Suddenly—I assure you, completely unexpected and not hoped for—I felt precisely that *Someone* stood beside me, Someone who radiated comfort and strength. And I heard, but without *sound* ... as clearly and distinctly as if someone had literally spoken to me:
>   'Do not despair, you are not alone, *I am alive.*'

The woman wrote that she had thought a lot about her experience. She thought she tended more to interpretations of the rational, reasonable kind. She felt that perhaps she may be sensitive. On the other hand, she felt repelled and embarrassed, even deterred, by religiously emotional scenes on television— such as she had seen once on TV in Maranata meetings.

And we continue to quote the woman's own words from the document:

> Mostly I tend to the 'explanation' (which really is no explanation at all) that it is true when in our service the words are spoken 'The Lord is near those who are of humble and troubled spirit ...'

The emphasis is on 'humble' and 'troubled'.

> My philosophy is this. Perhaps there are two realities — our reality
> and the other reality — which normally are separated by a wall, a wall
> that was erected by our own ego. Most of us are, perhaps *have to be*,
> quite egocentric and sure of ourselves to overcome daily worries, I
> guess, in order to be able to stand life in a world full of misery,
> sorrow and suffering.
>
> But in moments when the ego has lost all importance, when one
> feels to the bones 'my own strength cannot help', then there is no
> more wall. Then we can have contact with the other reality where
> Christ lives.

Christ appeared out of the dark

A retired man, born in 1901, described (Report No. 60) a Christ
vision he had had when he was 22 years old, during the year of his
high school graduation. He had been taken ill with rheumatic fever,
or possibly only with rheumatic pain; at times he felt compelled to
assume the former. The illness threatened his plans for the future. 'I
felt depressed and unsure . . .' The report continues:

> I will not describe my situation but just correctly report what hap-
> pened.
>
> During one of those nights I saw Christ appear out of the dark. A
> mild shine that could not be overlooked came from Him. He bent
> over me and my bed. He did not look like one of the traditional
> pictures of Christ. What struck me most was the power of His eyes:
> powerful and at the same time tender. Then the picture quietly
> disappeared towards the wall. But in the receding movement I
> noticed a strong admonition I interpreted as meaning 'Seek Me!'

In answer to prayer Jesus appeared

I was very sad. From all my heart I asked God for help, and I was
heard. Jesus appeared to me, and on a morning around Easter heard
what I had asked for.

A 75-year-old woman wrote this (in Report No. 8) without giving any details of the vision. However, she was able to date the experience exactly: Maundy Thursday, 1973, between 6 and 7 p.m.

The following is told in Report No. 5. A woman had experienced great sorrow and was continually reminded of it. She is a church-oriented Christian and used to pray each morning: 'Thank you God, for guarding and protecting me during the night.' Then the document reports of an auditory (or verbal) experience.

> During this difficult time my prayer had been repressed through all these sad happenings. One morning, however, just as I woke up, the words flashed through my mind 'Why don't you pray?' I was afraid. The words had come into my consciousness as fast as a lightning flash. But I answered: 'No, I am unable to pray, now when my mind is so preoccupied with all these sad happenings.' Then I clearly heard the words: 'Should I not be able to penetrate them? I, who have risen from the dead? Every time a light breaks through the darkness I rise again, the resurrection happens again.'

Your cure will proceed at a fast pace

Jesus is the physician.

Tradition has it that Jesus 'healed all the illnesses and infirmities from which the people suffered' (Matt. 4:23). According to Luke, chapter 9, Jesus even gave His disciples the power to heal the sick.

Quite a few of the documents that were sent to the Religious-Sociological Institute report of sudden cures; at least, one can learn from them the opinion of the reporting persons that they had received help in a miraculous way through having met Christ.

Report No. 49 speaks of an operation for kidney stones in the Värnamo Hospital in 1955. The operation had been complicated through a heart problem of the patient. She relates:

I lay there for a week; then Dr W. said, 'We have no choice. Would you like to have the operation?' With thanks I said yes. 'The risk is great,' said the doctor. The operation was successful. I lay in intensive care for two nights. After that I was moved to a room with four patients who seemed to have incurable illnesses. In the evening I lay there crying and thinking 'I probably won't come home again'.

The patient saw her illness in this way. Now to her experience:

I don't remember whether I had gone to sleep or not, but I heard clearly a voice, and I repeated the words I heard: 'Your wounds will heal at a fast pace.' I said, 'I thank you, Jesus.' With that I had received assurance that I would be able to return home. Joy returned to me.

According to the report another very ill patient in the same room had heard the woman speak and said, 'Where is this written in the Bible?' 'I answered, "I don't know. But I will try to find out when I come home." My brother and a sister of the congregation found it to be in Isaiah 58:8.'

In closing, she reported that many years later she had to go through another difficult operation. 'God is true; I survived that operation too.' The document closes: 'If you need proof that I speak the truth please ask at the hospital. They have the records there.'

The verse of Isaiah has the following wording: 'Then your light shall burst forth like the dawn, and you will be cured at a fast pace, and your fairness will walk before you, and the splendour of God bring up the rear of the procession.'

At the sickbed

One night I was wide awake, not sedated by injections or pills, when He was standing beside my bed.

In her terse report (No. 22) a patient said that this had happened in a hospital where she had had a difficult operation. And it says further:

A great unrest had taken hold of me. I survived the operation, came home and was healed. When I told my family about it they obviously laughed and were of the opinion that I have had a hallucination. But I, of course, know how it was, and I am happy to be able to live with my Master, and one day be allowed to die in His presence.

A woman from Denmark wrote the following (Report 51). She had lost her first child and was pregnant again. But then she became ill with malaria, a disease she had contracted when she had been in Malaysia and Thailand.

On Christmas Eve the fever came back. I was taken to the hospital into the maternity ward. I was given painkillers and was taken into a large room where I was all alone. The staff instilled courage into me, said I should not be afraid. A nurse came in with a dish of red soup, and I ate it—strange that I was able to do this.

After the operation I was wheeled back into the same room. The young doctor said something like, our child would not live. At this, I just saw black, was outside of space and time. Was I dead? I don't know.

But suddenly He was there. I saw Him come but didn't know who He was. He took with His left hand my right one and I was filled with a great joy I cannot describe in words. I felt such happiness, peace, joy, thankfulness. No words are adequate to describe this.

Together we walked on a green slope. It seemed, we walked up a mountain.

The woman lost her little son. 'He was a lovely boy, lived 18 days and then joined his older brother.'
But she still remembers the slope on the mountain.

I often go there and can feel the peace lingering which had filled my heart to such an extent. I long for Him who gave it to me, and I am looking forward to dying when my time comes.

A 60-year-old woman from Norway wrote (in Report No. 100) how she had seen Christ one evening in the Ullevåls hospital. She had been sickly for years and was interested in the phenomenon of faith healing. Among other things, she had observed a new interest in it in the Anglican Church. For years she had taken medications from health food stores, yet without success. On the evening she reports on, everything seemed to have collapsed for her. She had been taken to hospital with a fractured thigh bone, as she believed. She lay in bed in a lot of pain. She said she felt totally abandoned by God.

At that, she heard somebody coming, a figure approaching her. 'He was dressed in a long, white gown. He was tall and majestic.' He wore a dark blue overcoat 'with a hood hanging down His back, almost to the floor'. On His head was a shining, golden crown. 'Despite His kingly bearing and His sublime dignity an infinite compassion radiated from Him.' Later on the patient read in the book *Beyond Ourselves* by Catherine Marshall a description of Christ which she finds agreed completely with what she had seen. 'There was in Him a curious combination of kingliness and tenderness.'

The woman heard Jesus speak:

Today you have seen here many doctors and you know that there is one of them who calls himself 'Chief Physician'. But you must know that *I* (strongly emphasized) am the Chief Physician in this house, and this is my visiting hour. When the evening comes, the lights are turned down and sounds become less, then I make my rounds; for then I have the possibility to speak to the hearts. And to you I say: 'You are thirsty; I was thirsty too. You are feeling abandoned by God; it happened to me too. You have the cold iron in your flesh and blood; I had that too.'

Earlier the woman had described that she had been put into a stretching apparatus and that her leg was pierced below the knee with steel wire. The experience ends:

He did not say more; he turned around and was gone.

I felt such a joy that I could have jumped out of bed ... For I was not spoiled in such things. I was able to feel in my own body something of what He had done for all of us ... Perhaps I could have lost all my faith that evening had Christ not come to me.

2. 'This is My body!'

Christ Appears During the Communion service[5]

Once upon a time it happened in Jerusalem: the last Passover meal that Jesus spent with His disciples. Jesus had sent Peter and John ahead to prepare the meal in the Holy City. A large room in the upper storey would be assigned to them for a meal (Luke 22:12).

> And when the hour had come, He sat down at the table and the apostles with Him. And He said to them: 'I have waited with great longing to eat the Passover with you, before my path of suffering begins. I tell you: I will eat no more until it comes to fulfilment in the Kingdom of God.' And He took the cup and blessed it and said: 'Take this and share this draught among you. For I tell you: From now on I shall no longer drink of the juice of the vine until the Kingdom of God has appeared.'
>
> And He took the bread, blessed it, broke it and gave it to them and said: 'Take this, it is my body which is given for you. And always when you do this make my being come alive within you.' And after the meal He took the cup and said: 'This cup is the new covenant with God, established through my blood which is shed for you.' [Luke 22:14–20]

The New Covenant

Jesus Himself founded the meal which we call the Last Supper. St Paul stated this in his first letter to the Corinthians. At the same time he brought the words of Jesus in the context of his times.

> I received these words, as I handed them on to you, from the Lord Himself. In the night He was betrayed the Lord Jesus took the bread,

spoke words of blessing over it and broke it and said: 'Take this, it is my body! From now on, do this to make my being present.' In the same way, He took the cup after the bread had been eaten and said: 'This cup is the new covenant with God through my blood. Do this, whenever you drink from it, to make my being present.' [1 Cor. 11:23–5]

The Last Supper is a sacred act because Jesus Himself has founded it. Whoever celebrates the Last Supper takes part in a happening which goes over the world for centuries. In one of the prayers of thanks which is spoken in the Swedish Church after receiving the Last Supper are the words: 'Bestow on us the grace to celebrate the memory of Jesus on Earth in such a way that we shall be allowed to take part in the great Last Supper in heaven.'

The Last Supper is a holy moment because it conveys a meeting with Jesus Christ, the risen Lord. In bread and wine we receive the body of Jesus, sacrificed for us, and the blood of Jesus, shed for us. 'The cup of blessing over which we speak the words of consecration, does it not offer the communion of the blood of Christ? The bread we break, does it not offer the communion of the body of Christ?' (1 Cor. 10:16).

Christ comes into His congregation

In Matthew 18:20 we find an avowal which can be called the basis of every service of God. Jesus said: 'For where two or three are gathered together in my name, there am I in the midst of them.'[6]

So Jesus is present in the congregation where a service is being celebrated. Martin Luther tried to explain how this was possible. The words of the Creed—'Jesus sitting at the right side of the Father-God'—do not mean an image describing a space we call sky. When God resurrected Jesus from death all bonds binding to earthly life were broken. As described in the New Testament, the Apostles could experience how Jesus was able to reveal Himself suddenly, even come through locked doors, before His ascension into heaven. The risen, living Jesus shares in God's power. That is why He can be present wherever He wishes. He wants to be present where a service and Last Supper are celebrated, just as He had promised.

As God came into our world in the shape of Jesus Christ as the 'Son of God', so He continues to be near human beings by sending Jesus Christ. In this way Luther tries to make the presence of Jesus during the service understandable. In a commentary on the letter to the Galatians he speaks often of 'Christ's daily arrival': He always comes, in conformance with His avowal, into the congregation when the service is being celebrated.

Conversation with Jesus at the communion table

Folke Holmström, Theol. D., previously active as professor for systematic theology at the University of Lund and as lecturer for religious studies in Linköping and Lund, wrote in a note dated 12 May 1973:

> When I celebrate the communion service it is not uncommon that the spiritual attention is, so to speak, concentrated on a word of Christ from any of the Gospels that resonates in my ear, actuated for me personally, like a prayer for the day.

Folke Holmström then related an event he called: 'Dialogue at the Table of the Holy Communion':

> Sunday after St John's Day, 25 June 1972, at the communion service at Brunnby, surprisingly I came into close contact with the Redeemer in a for me undreamt of quality of experience. While the officiant, the minister of the congregation, Einer Annefors, was making his round distributing the Holy Meal, I found myself suddenly in an inner dialogue with Christ, with responses in the regular psalm rhythm. I had no vision of the figure of the Saviour. But although the voice

seemed to come from a weak luminescence in the background I had
no doubt that it was He who had the kindness to speak to me.

The content as well as the form corresponded to the well-known
and beloved Psalms Nos. 76 and 77 of Passiontide, both translated by
Erik Norenius (1675) in the same metre and rhythm, but now
transformed from praying to Jesus to an exchange of responses, to a
joyful exchange song between the soul and the Lord. I also had the
uncertain impression of an elastically extended time dimension since
during a few short minutes several verses could alternately be
exchanged.

When I returned to my seat in the church, beside my wife, I
immediately opened my psalm book. But strangely, I could not find
any agreement with the words of comfort that just now had sounded
in my inner ear; however, I was unable to reproduce these words in
my memory later on.

An invitation to participate in the communion

Those who took the initiative for this book received through
Bishop Helge Fosseus the following communication from a
woman who wished to remain anonymous. The description
relates an experience of Christ in the church of Onsala during the
year 1966, or '67. In the communication (Report No. 96) the following is emphasized: 'My experience stands as clearly and
distinctly before me as on the day it happened.'

It was unusual for her to have gone to church alone. The
quotation continues:

As many people walked forward towards the communion table I
remained seated. I thought: 'Today I will not go but wait for another
time.'

I sat on the right side in the church, one or two rows below the
gallery. I think another person sat towards the outside of me.

As I was sitting there, I saw a blinding light in the aisle in front
of my bench, about at the height of a person. From the left in front
of me I heard a voice saying the single word 'Christ'. It also

seemed as if someone was pointing to the light, as if to say who this was.

A moment later I heard the words coming from the light: 'Whoever does not eat and drink with me has no part in me.' Then everything was gone in a moment. I don't know whether this formulation is in the Bible and has been spoken by Jesus, but I remember it exactly word for word.

I got up in a hurry to go to the communion table and in doing so I looked at those who sat there unaffected. Therefore, they had not seen what I had seen. Often I have thought of this, but never have I told anybody about it. I kept it as a tender secret in my heart.

In such a poor way do we, most people, profess our faith in Christ, and are such cowards. After all, we should testify to the fact that we have Christ among us.

So far the note.

In John 6, the chapter reporting, among others, the Feeding of the Five Thousand, Christ speaks of the Bread of Life. Verses 48–56 have the following wording. In verse 53, below in italics, the wording comes close to the above mentioned words:

> Jesus answered to them: 'I am the bread of life. Your fathers ate the manna in the wilderness, and they died. This is the bread which descends from heaven. Whoever eats of it will not die. I am the life-giving bread which descends from heaven. Whoever eats of this bread will live through all cycles of time. And the bread which I shall give — that is my earthly body which I shall offer up for the life of the world.'
>
> Then the Jews argued among themselves and said, 'How can he give us his earthly body to eat?'
>
> Jesus answered, 'Yes, I tell you: *If you do not eat the earthly body of the Son of Man and drink His blood you have no life in you.* Whoever eats my body and drinks my blood has life beyond the cycles of time and I give him the power of resurrection at the end of time. For, My flesh is the true sustenance, and My blood is the true draught. Whoever truly eats My flesh and drinks My blood remains in Me and I in him.'

A priest experienced the presence of Christ

A priest of the Swedish Church sent us the following report. Since he expressly wished it to be treated confidentially his name will not be mentioned here (Report No. 90).

It was the Saturday after Easter (no year is given). He was alone at home. His family was away because of the funeral of a near relative. We quote from the report:

> On the following day the confirmation was to be celebrated. It was not my task to give the sermon but to help with the confirmation. Suddenly I noticed that something was happening; it was as if somebody was coming closer to me, but through closed doors. I saw nobody, heard nothing either. But more distinct than with all my senses I was feeling that somebody was with me and that this Somebody was Christ. His presence gave me, of all things, a clear certainty of the resurrection and its reality. The faith in it was overwhelming; it overcame me. I even smiled a little ... Was all this really so simple? It was as if all questions had been answered all at once, all problems solved. Life received a completely new form. Admittedly, I said to myself: 'All this cannot be just like this. Christ must have gone wrong. I am absolutely unworthy of such a thing.' But the doubt was only theoretical, was being caused by my brain. In my heart I was experiencing His presence as being the most obvious of all things ...
>
> As words from the Bible for next day's sermon, I had chosen the words of the Risen One to Thomas: 'Blessed are those who don't see but nevertheless believe.' Probably by habit I kept the concept drawn up before the experience. But it was almost a little humorous to speak of 'not seeing', despite the fact that I had not seen but had been surrounded by a clarity which was too bright to be grasped either by the eyes of the body or those of the soul.
>
> Of the service I remember only that it appeared as seemingly new although it took its course, as it usually did. The inner positivity, however, made its course appear indescribably bright to the members of the congregation.
>
> But it was only that I could not stand all this spiritual abundance:

no direct pain, but a feeling that the fragile vessel must burst from the golden treasure within it if this should continue. I remember that I repeated a word I had previously used when the burden and trouble were too much: 'I cannot bear it any longer, O Lord, let me go!' I did not have to wait in vain for my wish to be granted.

When I had proceeded to the altar together with my colleague it was my task to read the common prayer and the 'Praise be to You ...' As I was to go on to the words of the sacrament my pulse became irregular and my heartbeat became pronounced. I am pretty well used to such attacks. So I took it calmly. Otherwise I could have feared to fall down dead. At this instance, the condition had vanished as quickly as a lamp could be turned off. I noticed that my colleague turned to me as if to ask: 'What do you have in mind?' At that moment my voice came back, and without difficulty I took on my part of the liturgy and that of distributing bread.

The next day I had a visit of an old and pious lady. Without telling of my experience I tried to find out whether she had noticed my heart trouble. The answer was 'No'; but she mentioned that I had been like a 'different person'.

The informant then adds a few very personal comments which are worth being passed on. It is about how he reacted to his experience. He was unable to jubilate about his experience of salvation; that would have been a selfish falsification of what had happened, he said. He feels justified to quote psalm 18:47 maintaining the proper distance: 'The Lord lives: praised be *our* rock and praised be the God of *our* healing.'

The redemption is here, as part of the resurrection of Christ, and in this redemption I took part not thanks to a personal favour but just as I share in air, sunshine, life with all of humanity. The only difference is, while these elements reach all, I was shown the grace to be able to feel the nearness which touches many, without being noticed. When it becomes necessary to explain why I of all people was able to experience the redemption—in this objective, almost inescapable way which must have been similar to the way the certainty of pre-destination of Augustine, Luther, Calvin must have been—then I can find no explanation other than signified in the answer St Francis gave to the question why he had been chosen: 'Because none more unworthy could be found.' And now, afterwards, I find it significant that the text of the epistle I read for the first Sunday after Easter contains one of the shortest statements St Paul ever made about himself. He compares himself with a premature baby ...

'I saw the Saviour'

Among the notes that were sent to us a few are written in the form of a poem. One of these (Report No. 35) describes a vision of the living Christ at the communion table:

> I saw
> The communion table
> In one of our churches.
> I saw the miracle happening.
> I saw the Saviour
> Walking
> Between the two celebrants
> Laying
> His hand onto each guest at the communion table,
> Giving His blessing to them.

'I saw the Saviour.' A number of reports tell of just this experience: the living Christ at the communion table.

Report No. 138: a lay person, born in 1920, wrote to Gunnar Hillerdal in a letter dated 11 January 1973 the following (from the letter it does not become clear in which year this happened):

> In yesterday's paper I read an article about persons who had seen Jesus and who had contacted you. I read neither your book nor the advertisement, so I don't know their intention; but I shall tell of the event I experienced.
> It was in the Snöstorps church during communion after the confirmation of my son. I had just knelt at the ring around the altar. There a figure of light stood before me, a man in shining white

garments, His arms extended forward as if to receive me.

This I experienced for a while. Immediately afterwards I noticed how deeply moved I was.

I have told of this experience only to a few people. But for me it is *reality*.

A woman, over 80 years old (Report No. 31) said spontaneously she did not mind having her experience published, as long as her name was not mentioned:

It was many years ago, in 1946, in a small church in Värmland, on Maundy Thursday. The minister stood in front of the altar and invited the congregation to take communion. My husband and I had in mind to follow the invitation. Then something odd happened, completely unexplainable to an ordinary person like me, but nevertheless true. The priest disappeared and in his stead Someone stood there, radiant with light and more beautiful. I recognized Him. It was my Saviour. He looked exactly as I had seen Him years ago in the Bertel Thorvaldsen Museum: the extended hands, the tender look.

I believed I heard the wonderful words: 'Come to me, all of you who are in misery and burdened and I will refresh you.'

The wonderfully beautiful sight lasted only a few moments. But this was enough for me. And it is still enough, despite the many years that have gone by since I had this strange experience. This countenance is forever engraved on my retina. It has helped me often with various experiences during the changing years of life. It was before me in days of joy, in days of sickness and serious suffering, in days of sorrow that wore me down when the unbidden, rarely welcome, guest entered our home a short time ago and took my life's partner with him, leaving me behind.

3. 'Was it Christ who taught me my art?'

Wäino Aaltonen's dream vision

Early on in the book 'What Christ Taught Me', published in 1957, one can read a report by the Finnish artist Wäino Aaltonen who is known mostly for his sculptures. Quite sensationally the whole collection of experiences and documents is opened with the words: 'The question "What Christ taught me" I could answer with the short sentence: "Christ taught me to paint." This happened during a dream in 1912.'

Aaltonen described his dream:

I stood at home on our farm and started to paint. The landscape was very beautiful. As I looked around, the sky was full of colours. The pure, beautiful colours gradually grouped themselves into a gigantic figure of Christ. It was so clear, beautiful and colourful that it stands like that before my inner sense even today. The next moment I felt that Someone, firmly but in a friendly way, took hold of my right arm. I had the palette in my left hand and, as I looked up, Christ stood beside me. He took the brush from my hand, took some paint off my palette and started to paint. I looked on in astonishment, and in an instant it was completely clear to me how to work with paint. Once in a while Christ looked at me as if to ask whether I understood. I answered in the affirmative by silently nodding my head. Words were not necessary. This look Christ gave me was so all-knowing, all-encompassing and true that I cannot forget it as long as I live. Even today it lives completely in my soul. He kept painting until the picture was finished. Every shade of colour lay in harmonic beauty before my eyes. When the picture was finished Christ returned the brush to me and looked at me as if to ask whether I had understood. I nodded; but when I wanted to thank Him in full humility He was gone. A great feeling of fear transformed itself quickly into great joy: I had become master over the paints. Now I was able to use them as I pleased, within the methods of art.

Aaltonen reports further what strange consequences this dream vision has had. At that time (1912) he was studying in the third year at the Academy of Art in Abo. On the morning after the dream he went directly to the school and tore up the picture he had started. The teachers protested but could not stop him. 'They just did not know what I knew,' writes Aaltonen. When he then had painted a new picture he was at once called into the studio of Professor Westerholm.

My new picture stood there. Professor Westerholm said: 'Your picture has unheard of, beautiful colours.' He then was absorbed into every detail of the picture and asked me whether I saw the colours really in this way. Boldly I answered that I saw the colours as I wanted to see them. At that he asked me about the truth, the truth in nature. I cannot say where or how the words came to me as I answered: 'This is the truth in art.'

Wäino Aaltonen reports further that the dream and what happened in it went on standing alive before him. 'And besides, it has strongly influenced my spiritual development.'

'He explains water, fire and air'

In Report No. 82, sent to the Institute for Religious — Sociological Studies, one can read the following:

As an artist I am very sceptical in regard to outer 'looks'. We got to know the difficulties of perception and have discovered in the dilemma of the art of portraiture that how the outer looks shown are dependent on the one who sees them ...

Jesus Himself saw the innermost being of a person, his or her faith, and nowhere is reported that He ever spoke of the outer looks of a person. Presumably the way He saw was of quite a different kind, not of the usual one. Otherwise He would have deceived Himself and, therefore, also us.

The writer believed in a contact with Jesus.

I believe that His words and His voice are the innermost of the human voice. He gives me no grand explanations of the world, but He teaches me to understand the four elements. He explains to me the nature of water, fire, air and earth. He has illuminated me with the light that shines inside of us so that I cannot forget it. That was an experience of such blinding, penetrating light that the beaches of the continent faded in comparison so that I felt saturated with sun although it was autumn.

He taught me to understand the colours and to read the language of the light in the world of the senses. Patiently and without getting tired He explained everything to me. He has not forgotten the prayer I prayed in the evening when I was a child: 'Jesus, show Yourself to me when You think it is the right time.'

A picture takes on life

From Report No. 71 we reproduce the following:

In 1951 I started to carve a picture that was to portray Christ in the garden. But the wood crumbled and I stopped carving. I painted a few flowers and a fig tree. Then I kept the picture in a suitcase in the basement. Here it stayed until the end of October of 1972.

So, the work on the picture was taken up again during the autumn of 1972. The picture had been commissioned and was to be sold. The artist said, however, that during the work his interest in it became more and more intensive so that he decided not to sell the picture. He expressed this as follows:

All the time while I was painting the picture I felt sorry that I had agreed to sell it. When the picture was finished I stood it up against the door of the balcony and sat down on a sofa at the opposite wall.

Then it seemed to me that Christ's eyes and also His hands were moving. The flowers in the garden became alive. They had turned into human beings who surrounded Christ. Then I saw Christ sway from one side to the other. Oh, how He spoke! But I only perceived one word 'Gethsemane'. Lightning struck, and Christ disappeared in a light blue robe.

In His stead Mary sat there, covered in a red robe. She held a baby in her arm. She, and also the child, moved. A voice said: 'Christ has been born again'. Then I saw lightning again, and Christ stood there again as before. He spoke all the time. I saw His lips move, but now I could not hear any words. All this repeated itself several times. At one time it was Christ, then again Mary with the child.

Because the artist did not want to part with the picture he painted a second one. Then the transformation happened again. Again the picture became alive. But this time something beyond that happened:

In the centre, in front of me, stood a tall figure turning His back towards me. His snow white robe blinded me. I tried to look at His head, but I did not succeed; the light was too strong for my eyes.

Then He reached out with His right arm which was much longer than a normal man's arm. In His hand He held a few twigs, and I saw some thorns on them. I had the impression that this had to do with Christ's crown of thorns. But at this moment the twigs changed. He held a cross in His hand, approximately 70 cm (28″) long and 5 cm (2″) wide. It had rounded corners and looked like a grating of pure gold. A baby in nappies was tied to the cross. 'Christ who had been born again', this was the vision I experienced this time – but only a vision, I could not hear anything. The experience of this vision lasted a very long time.

'Christ led me into the garden'

Edith-Marie Gjers began to paint regularly only in 1969. Since then she developed an increasingly rich production of paintings inspired by Christianity. To the person reporting she expressed this in a letter in these words: 'It is Jesus with whom I study painting.' Art has taken on a meaning for her; through it she is able and willing to spread the message about the living, risen Christ.

'Morning, happy morning' was the theme of an exhibition she held on 15 April to 27 1973 in the church of Abrahamsberg. The motive is easy to see. On Easter morning Mary is looking for the Lord in the grave but finds Him alive. The exhibition was named after a line in the poem by Ylva Eggehorn 'Oh happy day', with reference to John 20:11–16:

> Morning, happy morning!
> Do not weep any more, Mary!
> Do not stand there and stare with vacant eyes
> At the grave's darkness, the emptiness, at death,
> He is not there!

Edith-Marie Gjers paints with bright colours. 'Hallelujah, He Lives' is a picture with the unusual proportion of 230 × 150 cm (7'8" × 4'11'). It is, as it were, an explosion of joy in strong colours. Her poem 'Eggehorn' sees Jesus come 'into the living garden, into the deep green, into the grass heavy with dew and flowers'. The whole sky is unbelievably blue from the morning wind, as He is coming, 'all light in His hands'. All this is like a commentary to the vision we meet in continual variations in Edith-Marie Gjers' work. The artist lets flowers jubilate, birds dance as if they were intoxicated. One hardly has to mention that her style is boldly expressionist. However, one could just as well speak of spontaneous, simple and naive art. The message cannot be overlooked. Its central, ever-recurring theme is 'The Garden of the Lord', also the title of one of her pictures. The motive of the flowering herb garden lets one think of the garden of pleasure in the Bible: as Christ shows Himself as the Risen One, earth and air are, as it were, transformed, at least for a few happy moments.

Edith-Marie Gjers talks about her inspirations

In an interview with Svensk Veckotidning (Report No. 3, 1973), Edith-Marie Gjers replies to a question about her background and earlier contacts with Christian preaching as follows:

I grew up in a Christian home. My parents belonged to the Mission Congregation. I myself joined the Pentecostal Church later on. But then so much else entered my life; I lost these contacts. Today I look back to these years as if I had slept through them.

From the article we learn that in later years there were particular experiences which later became a direct source of inspiration for Edith-Marie Gjers and her richly streaming art. Upon repeated requests she described the following experience:

It was 25 June 1969 — midsummer morning. I awoke early and felt an odd urge to paint. I got up, looked for the brush, paints, etc. I had not used them for years. I painted on anything handy. I felt an unheard of longing to express what had germinated for such a long time inside me. As I settled down I understood: what I wanted to do was not painting for painting's sake. No, what I longed for more and more was the urge to proclaim a message. People should gain through my painting. Then it was that Jesus appeared in my paintings. That irritated me and I wiped Him out. When I did this the pictures were no good, and I became ever more restless.

As Edith-Marie Gjers tells in the interview, this restlessness was connected with her own doubts. 'What did I get into? Am I worthy?'

In the report prepared for this book she continues:

I began to pray: 'O, Lord, help me to paint You as You are so that people can see You!'

One day in 1971 the following happened:

I stood and painted. It was midnight. I could not go to bed and leave the painting before I had become conscious of what the painting meant. At that, Jesus came and extended His arms. I hurried to paint Him, as long as He was there. That is how it happened that I promised to obey and not wipe Him out again when He wanted to be in the picture. It made me so happy that I could continue to paint. Now my art had meaning. Jesus led me into the garden. That was so wonderful. I wanted to stay there, experience the scent of this splendidly fresh morning. There He stood, full of life. The women who had searched for Him extended their hands and called: 'He is alive! He lives!' The birds jubilated, the flowers opened their blossoms, and everything breathed life.

So far the report of Edith-Marie Gjers.

How exactly did she experience the presence of Jesus at that time? And in which way did she feel the Christian inspiration when she painted her pictures? She answered direct questions about the night mentioned: then, in 1971, she had an intensive feeling of the presence of Jesus in her room. However, it was not a direct vision, in the sense of seeing the Master. She knew then and knows now that Christ was present in her room and that He made her His tool. In a way she cannot explain in more detail how she was inspired to grasp, to 'behold', what she had reported.

Edith-Marie Gjers does not make a secret out of her Christian inspiration. Jesus has become, as it were, her master teacher. 'I am in a school', and she is of the opinion that this school is also valid for the rest of her life. The experience of the presence is sometimes more, sometimes less distinct when she paints new themes which she, by the way, hardly chooses herself. But what happened then, at midnight, some time in 1971, was yet in her view something unique, a decisive moment, namely the hours when she felt Christ's presence especially strongly.

A living, risen Christ is the theme of the New Testament. Therefore, Edith-Marie Gjers does not find it to be something special that she had found her Master. She herself wrote: 'As He has shown Himself to His disciples and to the women so He wants to show Himself today, to me, to us, if we would only look and listen.'

'The Countenance', a report how a picture of Christ came about

A figure of Christ, carved in pinewood and about one metre (3½ feet) tall, is the eye-catcher for every visitor to the Östra Grav

Chapel in Jönköping. The artist is Margareta Engström, Bank-
eryd. She says in a 1972 interview about her work:

> Christ is a reality that comes to meet us! It is my will that people who
> come here in sad and dramatic hours of their lives can see and
> experience something lying outside the material life; that life is not
> over!

More and more over the years, Margareta Engström's oeuvre
contained sacred art. Until now she was known especially as a
sculptor. She has worked with many themes: 'Mother and child',
'Mary' appear again and again, and also, directly or indirectly,
the theme of Christ. She calls one sculpture 'Messiah'. It was
shown in The Green Palette in Stockholm in 1966. For the small
church in Ekenässjön the artist created another sculpture of
Christ; she named it 'My Kingdom is not of this World'.

When one visits Margareta Engström's studio one of her pictures immediately draws one's attention. She does not want to
sell it, and only reluctantly does she give permission for lending
it to an exhibition because the presence of this picture in her
studio is important to her. The picture has a special history of
coming about. From the beginning, the artist called it 'The
Countenance'. The visitor experiences the picture immediately
as a portrait of Christ. After hesitating for a long time, the artist
agreed to write down what happened as she was painting it.

> One day I was in the process of preparing for a work commissioned
> for a long time. At that moment I felt the presence of Somebody
> standing close behind me at my right. I felt I was gliding into a
> timeless condition of infinite tranquillity and quiet joy. Without
> hesitation, I went about the studio gathering tools and materials
> needed. I did not think of what I would need. Everything came to me
> in an obvious way despite the fact that I would begin to use a
> technique completely new to me. I placed a wooden board on the
> easel and started to work. I believe I had a pencil, some pieces of
> pastel, sandpaper and paints. I worked intensively and was sure that
> every movement of my hand was correct. I knew I would do this that

way and that another way. There was no uncertainty, no searching. I was in a condition of unheard of certainty, and yet I was conscious of the fact that this was nothing contrived or invented or intellectually calculated.

During the whole time I led, as it were, a wordless conversation with Him who stood behind me and whom I obviously regarded as Christ. It was as if time and space and all were the picture which was coming into being. I cannot say that I felt Someone holding or leading my hands. I felt myself to be in a condition where it streamed from Him (behind me) through my hands into the picture; and I knew that it was His countenance that was being created.

How long did I work? I don't know. But afterwards, as the studio and time re-entered my consciousness—it had become evening—I saw the countenance on the wooden board and got scared. Was it possible that Christ Himself had come into the studio to visit me? I had turned my back to Him and had only worked. No, perhaps someone else who was near to Him had been here, because someone certainly had been here.

Visitors recognize Christ

Out of this uncertainty Margareta Engström decided to name the picture 'The Countenance', without indicating that she herself had had the feeling that Jesus Christ had been present and had inspired her work. She wrote that she would think it presumptuous to speak of a picture of Christ.

Her next of kin, her parents, viewed the picture first and spontaneously thought it was a portrait of Christ. Margareta Engström reports that they were astonished about her hesitation because earlier she had not made her Christian orientation a secret when she called two of her pictures 'Messiah' and 'Christ'.

'Many have been touched by this picture', the artist reports. She especially mentions a woman she had promised not to identify. The woman herself has had a vision of Christ, which Margareta Engström had written down according to her report.

She described the situation like this. The woman was resting and was busy in her mind with daily problems. Then she saw Jesus:

> Suddenly He stood there in my room ... so obvious and clear, a wanderer with mild, fine eyes, brown hair and a coat that fell in folds about His shoulders. He looked so dear; His eyes were mild and good. A gentle smile played around His mouth. I had the feeling that we were old friends, and I wanted to smile back at Him. A bubbling, hot joy of life rose in me, peace and joy I had never known like that before.

The woman ended her report by saying that Christ is there and that she can rely on Him. But afterwards she wondered how she was able to see Jesus so distinctly, 'because I had my face covered with a newspaper'.

The Christ picture which this woman had seen looked exactly like Margareta Engström's picture 'The Countenance'. 'The picture in your studio, the face on the wooden board, is an exact portrait of Him — that's what He looked like.'

4. The Face and the Figure

In this chapter it shall be brought to the attention of the reader how Jesus was experienced by those who have written and reported what they have seen and heard or perceived in other ways.

Deliberately we have collected and categorized the text by themes. With some it is about a total picture, a characterization of the whole figure. Other texts deal with less encompassing, yet perhaps just as fascinating themes: the countenance or eyes of Jesus, His voice, His hand that takes hold of someone or lays itself on their forehead.

The testimonies must speak for themselves. In some cases where we point out the artists directly we proceed with careful consideration. Also, we interpret, where possible and suitable, any motives or themes with a biblical background.

'How I saw Him', described by artists

In Report No. 77 an appearance in a dream was related. The writer reported:

> For me Jesus appeared in about the same way artists have portrayed Him, with a white garment and the gentle, beautiful face. And, I believe, Jesus looks like that.
>
> Around His head I saw a glory which was more beautiful than one can imagine because it was interwoven with a wreath of roses. And the wonderful thing is that it seemed to me that the roses were somehow alive. This was a picture of incomparable beauty ... His countenance radiated an outer and inner beauty which was not of this world but belonged to the beyond. A sweet fragrance, a scent streamed from the wreath of roses, as could not be found on this

Earth. He looked as we know it from pictures of the old masters of the fifteenth to sixteenth century. But mark you, this was a living face that smiled and spoke to me with His eyes.

In Report No. 73 a man spoke who expressly asked to remain anonymous. From the report one can gather that the writer knows a lot about art and works as an artist himself. He emphasized that about 20 years ago [1953], he immediately got up and tried to paint what he had seen.

> But I was not able to bring into reality the beauty that radiated from the appearance. The sketch still exists, and a year ago [1972] I made a stained glass window as a memory of the visit of the Master of Nazareth.

The picture of Jesus in art has undergone change. In the West, among others, the type was cultivated that was called *Majestas Domini* or *Rex Gloriae*, the majestic Lord Christ, King of Honours. An almond-shaped halo surrounds Jesus who sits on a rainbow, His right hand extended in a gesture of blessing, His left hand holding the globe. In the early Middle Ages a Majestic King is common. Instead of a crown of thorns Jesus has a real crown on His head. And while in the later Middle Ages Jesus is portrayed as the crucified, suffering human being, in many places the picture of the majestic Jesus lives on. It is difficult to say whether the reporting person thinks of specific artists when he speaks of old masters of the fifteenth or sixteenth centuries. The statement of historic times can of course be incorrect. The Majestic Jesus in art becomes, as it were, timeless; the theme returns continually.

The wreath of roses as a theme fascinates and can help us define a painting closely. Albrecht Dürer (1471–1528) painted the so-called *Feast of the Rosary* for an altar in Venice after he had received strong impressions on a journey through Italy (1505–6). The Polish sculptor Veit Stoss (1533) used the wreath of roses as framing of his *Salutation of the Angels* in the St Lorenz Church in Nuremberg. At some time in the Middle Ages a tradition was born to distribute roses when, halfway through Lent, the Sunday called *Laetare* was celebrated which was also called 'Rose Sunday' according to ancient tradition. The theme of that Sunday is 'Jesus, the Bread of Life'.

Just like Thorvaldsen's Christ!

In Report No. 18 we are told of an appearance in the sky.

> About 18 years ago [in 1955] I observed a radiant cosmic figure in the shape of a human being with His feet on the earth and His head in the zenith. Although the appearance vanished after a few seconds, it had been very distinct. Through the light that made up the folds of the garment I saw what was behind it. This was by no means a hallucination or fantasy. It happened on a Sunday between 11 and 12 o'clock. The figure showed a similarity with the Christ statue the great Danish sculptor Thorvaldsen had created after what he is said to have seen.

Report No. 104 speaks of an unpleasant experience in connection with a flirtation in 1935. A woman — then 20 years old — sat in a pub in Dresden together with a significantly older man. The situation showed signs of becoming unpleasant. She reports:

> Then I distinctly felt that Somebody stood behind me on the left. Spontaneously I turned around, and what did I catch sight of: Christ! I turned quickly again to look at the table, played with my beer glass and thought: 'Something is not right with you, but you didn't drink that much that it would give you hallucinations.' Then I turned around again, this time slowly and deliberately. He was still standing there. He looked like Thorvaldsen's Christ.

She said she has thought and brooded about it many hundred times; 'thought about and prayed'. Then she declared:

> I did not ask myself whether Christ had really been there. Although I had tried to shake off the experience, to deny it, I nevertheless knew the whole time that it had been reality itself. But I have asked: 'Why Thorvaldsen's Christ? And why at all?' Gradually I received the

answer: 'So that you would recognize Me and would not deny Me.' I have totally forgotten everything else around this experience, for instance how we had got into this pub and how we got out of it again; what was its name and where in Dresden was it located. But today I can still see very clearly in my mind the smoky room, the seating arrangement among other seats and Christ—Thorvaldsen's!—to the left in the aisle behind me, which ran through the whole pub. And my Thorvaldsen's Christ was not a stiff, dead Jesus made of plaster of Paris. He moved His hands, lifted them about 20 cm (8"), a little less to the front. Unfortunately I cannot draw; otherwise I would make an exact sketch of it all.

The Danish sculptor Thorvaldsen through his statue of Christ known to, and loved by, millions of people seems to have strongly influenced the picture of Christ. The opinion arose that this work of art would remind one of works by Raphael, especially in respect to the accomplished and beautiful lines. Thorvaldsen's copy of Christ shows a powerful sovereignty, a statue of an ideal with a mild countenance and the open hands of the Redeemer.

Interesting are the words of our witness: 'Not a stiff, dead Jesus made of plaster of Paris.' Critics said of Thorvaldsen's art— as, for instance, in the characterization by Volke Holmér and Lars Eric Åström in the Swedish Encyclopedia—that the idealistic beauty and abstraction of his art often contain a negative trend, something soft and bloodless.

'So indescribably beautiful'

On 9 September 1971, a then 66-year-old woman experienced a Jesus vision (Report No. 61). A near friend of hers conveyed her impressions 'as well as possible word for word' through a tape recording. The woman was dependent on a wheelchair and had prayed imploringly for help. On that day she had attended the funeral of a friend and had felt that granting of her prayers was near. In the evening the following happened:

Suddenly the room became bright in an unprecedented way ... It was so bright that the eyes hurt. It radiated from the centre of the room. A brightness without comparison radiated from the lamp at the ceiling, spread out in all kinds of beautiful beams as from a star. In the midst of these beams Jesus was standing, fully alive. His robe had an indescribably beautiful bluish colour. On one shoulder it was cream coloured, on the other pink. On His feet He wore sandals with only one strap. The hair was chestnut brown. On His back the coat was of a beautiful light blue.

In Report No. 45 another woman spoke of a similar experience.

His divine figure was so blindingly beautiful that words are too poor to describe it. He wore a radiantly white garment which was drawn together at the neck and fell down along His figure in rich folds. He was beardless. The nose was quite large, but the whole countenance was of a wonderful beauty. The eyes were big and velvety brown, uncommonly good and tender, and they seemed to penetrate my whole being.

Another woman related in Report No. 69 that she had seen Jesus in heaven. She wrote:

He looked just like He does on most paintings: with long open hair that falls over His back and shoulder, and with a long garment that reaches the feet.

Do we know how Jesus dressed?

It is reported to us in John 19:23 that the soldiers, after having crucified Jesus, took His clothes and divided them into four parts, one for each soldier. The text continues: 'Then they also took the cloak. This cloak was seamless, woven in one piece from top to bottom.' So they cast lots for it. In the Swedish Bible translation the coat is called 'body-coat', 'shirt-coat' or 'shirtlike garment', which was worn directly on the body. This garment — *tunica* in Latin — could be quite long; it was gathered up by a rope or belt. The coat was of coarse wool or, if it was of a higher quality, of finer wool or of linen. The other main garment, during the time of the New Testament—surely was the overcoat. Even the poor wore one. (Compare, for instance, Mark 10:50 or Exodus 22:26-7, the instruction to return before sunset an overcoat taken as security.) This overcoat was both raincoat and protection against the cold. A sleeping person could wrap himself up in it, like he would in a blanket.

More particulars about clothing are not available in the New Testament. However, a few passages in the Bible report of the overcoat of Jesus. When Jesus had stilled the storm on the Sea of Galilee and had gone ashore with the disciples, it says that the people knew Him and brought the sick to Him. 'And they asked Him to be allowed only to touch the hem of His garment. And those who touched it were completely healed' (Matthew 14:36). The Roman soldiers of the governor in the Praetorium stripped Jesus and put a purple robe on Him (Matt. 27:28).[7]

'A shining light as I have never seen one before'

A man from Denmark who has read in Danish newspapers of the research of the Religious-Sociological Institute sent in a report (No. 47). In the introduction he says that he believes in God but is 'not religious', an expression which by itself would be worth a sociological investigation. From the report it follows that the appearance happened after the evening prayer:

> In the evening I lay in bed and had prayed the Lord's Prayer and a prayer from my childhood: 'Good Jesus, plead for me, lead me into heaven so that I can live with You in peace and eternal quiet. Let me love You forever, You who shed Your blood for me on Golgotha.'
>
> When I had said 'Amen' then suddenly brightness surrounded me, the kind of which I had never seen before. Suddenly Jesus stood beside my bed. Then I became aware of a power so great that I was feeling paralysed. He looked at me. I could not clearly see how He

looked, just that He had dark, but not long hair. He gave me a smile and was gone. All this took only a few minutes. I got up and immediately wrote down this miracle. It happened at midnight between 12 and 1 o'clock.

Our witness then added:

I brooded much about what had happened to me because I never had believed in miracles. But now I believe. I often questioned myself whether this had been Jesus because He was always portrayed in long hair. But later I received an explanation for the earthly features in His face. An American professor had found out that Jesus never had worn His hair long. That it had been Jesus I had seen I am convinced of. My Jesus presented me with a smile. For this I am thankful to Him for as long as I live. There is no doubt that there is life after death.

The light is a recurring theme in the New Testament. Jesus speaks of Himself as of the light: 'I am the Light of the World' (John 8:12). Purely physically Jesus is surrounded by radiant light during the transfiguration. 'His countenance shone like the sun, and His garments became shining white like light itself' (Matt. 17:2). A shining cloud overshadowed the disciples (Matt. 17:5) who are with Him on the mountain. 'God is Light,' writes John (1 John 1:5) and 'already the true Light is shining' (1 John 2:8). In the prophecy of a new heaven and a new Earth it says that the sun and moon do not need to lighten the city 'because the revelation of God enlightens it, and its lamp is the Lamb' (Rev. 21:23).

A smiling Jesus

A man who belongs to a Free Church congregation not named in the report wrote and reported how at age 25 he saw Jesus in the hall of the Free Church congregation at the occasion of a singing rehearsal (Report No. 17).

A few weeks before his experience the man was conscious of

the nearness of Jesus while he made a confession. 'Something entered into my innermost being that had not been there before.' About two weeks later he took part in a singing rehearsal. Fifteen 'brothers' sang together: 'Where I walk in the woods, on mountains, in valleys a Friend follows me, I hear His voice.' The last verse of the well-known song ends: 'Let me rise, dressed in Your garment, redeemed and blissfully calling at Your appearance: O my Lord and my God'. During these closing words the man saw an appearance that, according to his description, was only seen by him; but from the description one can get the impression that it was perceived by all the others.

> Very clearly I could see Jesus standing in the hall below, His whole figure as He extended His hands and arms towards us. His whole smile was visible to us ...

From the somewhat unclear text it follows that Jesus wore a coat that reached down to the floor.

> My experience was so spiritual that I could not sing; I just stood there, cried and looked at Jesus. When the singing had ended I told the others what I had seen. It was as if a stream of spirit wafted through us all which we will never forget. Yes, God is good; He presents us with meeting Him here on Earth. Since I have seen Him with my own eyes it is much easier for me to live and to pray to Jesus.

In Report No. 73 a man who works as an artist reports that he met the 'Master of Nazareth' during a night:

> His countenance took leave of me with a wonderful smile. Then the image vanished, quietly and almost imperceptibly, in the same way it had appeared.

'At first I thought it had been Judas ...'

A woman belonging to a congregation in Stockholm submitted the following report (No. 18) with details which differ from the usual descriptions of Jesus:

It was about midnight. I lay awake on my sleep-sofa in the living room. The figure stood there, very clearly ... First I believed it was a disciple of Jesus.

I thought He looked somehow ugly. That's why I first thought of Judas. But I quickly recognized my error. When I felt it was Jesus He approached me and I could see His eyes. They cannot be described, so wonderful, so loving they were. He knelt beside my bed and looked at me. He was of small build, had coarse features, a finely built body, shoulder-length brown hair falling down on both sides of the centre parting. His coat was crimson red, of a red colour I had never seen before. But this colour was a little muted and tended towards blue. A white shirt could be seen around the neck. He smiled. At that I could see His teeth. They were all there but a little off-colour.

A small detail in the report: was Judas really ugly? The New Testament says nothing about this. But his betrayal appeared to the first Christians not only inconceivable but also somehow as abominable. His death is described as repulsive: (Acts 1:18),[8] 'He fell forward and burst open in the middle, so his entrails gushed out.' 'Satan entered into Judas' (Luke 22:3)[9] – did that not have to have consequences? The reward for his betrayal was a shameful death. In this regard there are no limits to the imagination. Already in the early Church his body was described as disfigured and ruined.

But all this points more to our human need to find a scapegoat and imagine some details; historic evidence of this cannot be found in the New Testament.

However, we have cause to come back to the questions of Jesus' looks. There has come to us, also from the early Church, a tradition which describes Jesus not as beautiful but as ugly.

'This gaze, I will never forget it'

Report No. 25, written by a man, 64 years old, tells of having met Jesus in 1926 or later. He mentions that in that year he received a 'baptism in the Holy Spirit'. He did not feel healthy and — at his work place in a storage cellar — prayed urgently for help and recovery. Then he experienced the appearance of Jesus.

> A stream of joy penetrated me, and at the same time I saw Jesus stand before me, His hands lifted as if He wanted to say 'I am the Healer', but He said nothing. His appearance was like a clear figure of light with an infinitely keen, penetrating gaze. At the same time infinitely great love streamed from His eyes. So especially His eyes were what captivated me, and they were so full of love. Words cannot describe this. But His love appeared to me to be as infinitely great as the ocean is when one cannot see land, as if He wanted to say with His arms and hands and eyes: 'Oh, if only the whole world would come to Me, I would receive them all!.'

Report No. 4 conveys an experience of the year 1941 when the informant was a girl of almost 16 years of age. One evening, at about 9:30, she saw Jesus' countenance; it was surrounded, as it were, by a cloud. She did not see the whole figure, only the face and the shoulders.

> He looked at me. In His gaze I read nothing but condemnation. Never had I thought I was sinful. After all, I had gone to Sunday school and had learned that all human beings were sinners and that Jesus had the guilt of all of us taken on Himself. On the other hand, I had not sinned on purpose. I did not know of any fault of mine I would have to blame myself or feel remorseful for.
>
> His gaze had the effect that I saw myself with His eyes. Now I recognized that I was not only sinful but was nothing but sin throughout. When I saw my sin and realized that it was His mercy I was lacking I discovered that the condemnation was gone. Now His eyes radiated profound love, an inconceivable sea of love.
>
> I will never forget this look. When I saw it He said: 'I have given my life for you. Do you want to give yours for Me?' My reaction to this question was that I did not want to die. I was still so young. Then He said: 'Will you go where I would send you?' I thought He meant going as a missionary. In my simplicity I thought: I cannot speak other languages and don't know what is written in the

Bible. At that He said: 'Whom I call I also make capable.' Then He was gone.

In regard to her reaction, the woman continues:

I got up out of my bed and fell on my knees. I could not pray because I had never done so with my own words. Besides, what does someone say who has just met God? I only cried silently. I was not capable of thinking in words.

In Report No. 62, a 55-year-old man wrote he was a 'regular labourer', not a 'dreamer type despite my name' — the reporting person's first name is Joseph and obviously he was thinking of Joseph who interprets a dream in Genesis chapter 41. 'My friends think I have no nerves.'

In 1935 [at 18] the man, a member of the 'Swedish Mission Church' goes into a church. He is all alone in a small prayer room.

I knelt down and prayed to the King of kings. To use the language of the Free Church, I did not feel any direct 'open' contact in prayer although I know that it is always there. Suddenly I looked at something I will never forget. Clearly and distinctly, I could see Jesus. He carried a small lamb in His arm. I don't want to try to describe what I saw. All Jesus pictures I know of faded [in comparison]. But I want to mention His eyes: so tender and full of love, but at the same time so penetrating. Dear reader, you will understand me when I suggest the song No. 53 in our hymn book 'Most beautiful Lord Jesus, King of all, Son of God and Son of Man'.

In regard to several of the quoted statements one could ask for the New Testament background. Does the New Testament relate a statement or episode describing His gaze, His eyes as important? The New Testament does not describe the outer appearance; in vain do we look for direct descriptions. Yet it is possible to emphasize a few words or situations interesting to the reader of the Bible.

Jesus was able to look around in anger. When He had a dispute with the scribes, Mark says expressly: 'Then He looked around in anger, sorrowful about the stubbornness of their hearts ...'

When one reads the New Testament it can be assumed that Jesus was able to see directly what went on inside the souls of the people. Quickly He saw through the woman at the well (John 4), the rich youth (Luke 18), Pilate who tries to interrogate Him but soon becomes uncertain.

Was there something penetrating in the gaze of Jesus? The scene of the denial of Peter indicates that Peter lies for a third time. 'At that the Lord turned and looked at Peter', says Luke. And Peter 'went and wept bitterly outside' (Luke 22:61–2).

In Mark 10:21 we can read what happens during a conversation when a rich man asks Jesus for the way to eternal life. The man speaks of the commandments he tries to comply with. 'Then Jesus looked at him and loved him ...'

Jesus looks with loving eyes from the cross to His mother and wants to look after her. When Jesus saw His mother stand beside the disciple He loved, He said to His mother: 'Woman, see, that is your Son!' Then He said to the disciple: 'See, that is your mother!' And from that hour the disciple took her to himself' (John 19:26–7).

In all these scenes it was about Jesus on Earth. A strange passage in the Old Testament (Genesis 16:13) says: 'You are the God who sees.' Jesus Himself says: 'Whoever sees Me, sees Him who sent Me' (John 12:45).

Even the disciples who experience the risen Lord are amazed and moved by what happens to them. They experience that the Master sees them anew, looks at them with a loving gaze. He who shows Himself even to the doubting Thomas ...

'The Countenance was not uncommon, except for the eyes'

Report No. 92: a business man, 61 years old, had a vision of Christ on 22 December 1972, around 7 p.m.

Apparently he has had a tempestuous life—'I was a man of action in the world'—and more than 20 years earlier he had become a Christian. Near the end of 1972 he got into difficulties, which he described briefly as well as the struggle for the faith they led to.

A Christian too was exposed to temptations of various kinds, and at certain times they can get really noticeable. And so it happened to me during the week before Christmas of 1972. I had read in the book of Job what he had to suffer. I had read this often; but now it became clear to me that God's love had not been so great, as far as Job was concerned, especially at the beginning of his life's story.

This made me feel really disappointed. When I told my wife about it she said: 'You should pray to Jesus for help.' I did that. That was on 22 December 1972, at half past four in the afternoon. Then I read the newspaper and looked through my business papers. At seven o'clock I went into my room and lay down on my bed. I was thinking of work that had to be done. Now it was ten past seven. It was dark in the room. I was not tired at all, was wide awake. (Normally we never go to bed before eleven o'clock.) I never even dreamed of the Lord revealing Himself to me; I never have had such an experience before.

Suddenly I saw a countenance in front of me, in spite of the darkness in the room. The face was about 50 cm (1'8") away from me, was about 20 cm (8") high. I saw it in semi-profile. The hair was of medium length (so was the beard), and it was of a brown colour. I saw everything so clearly, even the pores of the skin and the individual hairs on the head and beard although it was dark in the room. I had no fear during the vision; on the contrary, a feeling of security came over me. The image was not like in a dream or like a photograph. It was alive, objective and outside of myself.

I have tried to describe the face. Nothing of it was uncommon except the eyes. Oh, these eyes, they radiated love, like a sea of love. And it must have been this love God wanted to show to me. Since that time I cannot doubt God's love to us, His children . . .

This appearance lasted a minute at the most. Then it vanished, but not suddenly but softly, like the lights in a hall gradually fade.

'A Golgotha vision'

Report No. 9 conveys a Golgotha vision. It is a woman who wrote. She told me in greater detail about the situation in which she found herself. She had the experience in her home in the early 1960s.

> I saw a group of shabby people, how they drove a man and forced him to carry a cross. Everything happened very quickly. I saw myself in this group, but from a distance. Then I saw Christ on the cross. He had to suffer much. The crown of thorns wounded Him so much that the blood dripped down. Then it happened that in desperation I sank down at the foot of the cross. And then the miracle happened: Jesus turned His head, looked into my eyes and smiled. His gaze was full of unearthly love to all human beings and of kindness without limits. This gaze went through my whole being, and a great happiness streamed through me. Then the appearance was gone.

'Never have I seen such eyes in a human being'

> It happened about 35 years ago [1938]. I sat in church, in the corner of a pew, close to the centre aisle. The pews have doors. I sat stooped forward and prayed. Suddenly I saw a figure stand in front of the door of the pew. He said clearly: 'Follow me'. Then he was gone. I cannot describe how He looked. That was unimportant, considering His wonderful eyes; big, dark, of inexpressible kindness and love. Neither before nor after this have I ever seen such eyes in a human being. Also, I never saw a picture in which an artist was able to paint these eyes.
>
> The memory of this gaze which rested on me followed me all these years, and I like to believe that I will be allowed to meet them again when I depart from the life on earth.

This beautiful description is from a now [in 1973] 70-year-old woman. She added:

How did I know it was Jesus I saw? I don't know. I asked myself: 'Could it not have happened like that when the disciples saw Him after the resurrection?' He came all of a sudden and also disappeared in the same way.

In Report No. 54 another woman wrote of a Jesus vision:

Such a beautiful figure in a blue coat and with eyes I cannot and don't want to ever forget. Such kind, radiant eyes; no human tongue has words for them.

In Report No. 35 a woman told of a peculiar experience she had on Epiphany day, 1961. Together with a servant she was lighting all candles on the candlesticks in the kitchen of the rural estate.

Then I saw suddenly big stars light up. They glittered and twinkled in such commonplace areas as the kitchen cabinet. In almost blinding light the Christ figure appeared.

The woman formed her experience into a poem which starts:

Out of the white emptiness of the mirror on the door
I suddenly saw a figure come out.
I saw His eyes.
They were so rich,
Not similar to any I have seen before.
His eyes were love and grace.
They bore witness of God.

In this report, as well as in the previous one, the main emphasis was on experiencing Jesus' eyes. Perhaps one can add that the peculiar mention of the door could remind one of certain words in the Bible. When Jesus speaks of Himself as of the Good Shepherd the theme of the door recurs several times. He who enters through the door is a shepherd of the sheep (John 10:2). 'Yes, I say to you: I am the door to the sheep' (John 10:7). 'I am the door. He who enters through me shall find salvation' (John 10:9).

'I will never forget His voice. He called me by my name'

In Report No. 43 a woman told of an experience which was for her 'so great and holy' that she has spoken of it only to very near friends until now. She was nursing her older sister who suffered from arteriosclerosis. Often during the night the sister was very restless, and caring for her was hard and tiring. But the thought of sending her own sister into a nursing home seemed to be an impossible one for her.

> One evening I could not find any words for praying. But all my inner being was one single request for help. Around 4 o'clock in the morning I awoke from a voice speaking in low tones, but clearly: 'I know that you are having a difficult time ...' [Here she was called by her name which we omit] 'but I will help you.' When I opened my eyes to see who was there I saw that it was Jesus. But then He disappeared in a cloud.
>
> I cannot say what He looked like. He appeared to me as a figure of light. But His voice, I will never forget it. And that He had called me by my name! That had become an immense help to me throughout the following year.

A tender voice

> Then I heard a tender voice saying to me: 'Why do you not want to leave everything and follow me?'

This Report (No. 19) says that the voice came during the night after the person woke up. An earlier hearing experience which was not described in detail had happened one evening during a service in a Free Church.

Report No. 77: Jesus came to a man in a small cabin in the forest during the night of 4 to 5 April 1934, during a 'dream vision':

> ... Then He spoke in a beautiful voice the words 'Be not afraid, just believe!'

What does the New Testament say about Jesus' voice? Directly, hardly anything. However, it would be reasonable to remind ourselves of certain situations: Jesus' words at the Feast of the Tabernacles were recorded in John 7:37–8: 'On the last, the great day of the festival Jesus stood there and called out loudly: 'Whoever thirsts, let him come to Me and drink! Whoever fills himself with my power through faith, from his body shall flow streams of life-bearing water.'

It would also be good to think of John's report of Jesus' speech. Jesus speaks of Himself as the good shepherd. In John 10 it says: 'He who enters through the door is a shepherd to the sheep. To him the doorkeeper opens, and the sheep hear his voice, and he calls his own by name and leads them out. And when he has brought them out he goes before them, and the sheep follow him, for they know his voice' (John 10:2–4).

'I feel distinctly His hand touching me'

In Report No. 98 a teacher told of an experience on an evening in 1949 when she was alone in a remote school house of a small village in the woods. 'It was such a strange evening: full moon and a violent gale.' The woman was used to being alone and was not afraid. She sat down at the harmonium and played and sang Thomas Kingo's choral 'Sadness and joy, they travel together'.

> Suddenly it seemed that I heard a knock at the house door downstairs. Maybe someone of the neighbourhood felt compassion for me. I went down to open, but nobody was there.

During this strange weather the woman went to the window and saw the clouds racing across the sky. At that she thought of a poem by Hjalmar Gullberg:

> I dream I hear someone knocking
> Softly on the door.
> I run downstairs.

How did You come here?
What kind of time is this?
What happens to the room I live in?
Does Your path of suffering
Lead here
Across the marketplace through side streets?

The report goes on:

> When I had spoken the poem Somebody came into my room.
> Instantly I knew who He was. I sank to my knees at the window and
> did not dare to turn around and look at Him. From Him streamed
> such light and such peace! They were beyond all reason. I felt dis-
> tinctly His hand touching me when He bent down to take a burden
> away from me, the burden that I was not good enough to be His
> instrument. How long I had spent on my knees at the window sill I
> don't know.

When she finally stood up and opened her eyes the moon
shone into the empty room and filled it with clear light (she had
just moved in and had not furnished her rooms yet). On the wall
she saw a black cross, the shadow of the wooden window frame.

> But outside the window this cross changed into another cross that
> was bright and reached up to the sky. His voice explained to me the
> mystery of the cross. I did not hear a voice, but in a way full of
> wonder the meaning of the cross became clear to me. The theme of
> sacrifice had been so difficult to comprehend for me. But now, I
> believe, I understood at once the meaning of Christ's deed of sacri-
> fice and its meaning for every human being. A powerfully great
> perspective opened up. I saw the cross between heaven and earth
> like an axle around which everything turns, the innermost mystery
> of creation, the Divine Love ...

'For a moment Somebody stayed between my friend and me'

A nurse reports (in Report No. 63) an appearance of Christ that
happened on a winter evening of 1940 or '41. She had travelled to

her home town and visited a school friend of old. One evening they sat in front of a burning fireplace and spoke of God. Her friend urged her to quote something which could strengthen her faith. In the following report the emphasis is on the experience of the gaze of Jesus. The remarkable feature of this report is that the friend, according to her own words, felt that something unusual had happened, although she did not see Jesus.

> I was looking for words, leaned back on my chair, felt very tired. The tongue did not want to form any words. From the dark dining room behind me something came. Like fire it went through me. I could not turn my head. I looked straight ahead past the table. For a moment Somebody stood at my side. Although my gaze was directed straight ahead I saw a figure in a garment full of folds. The eyes, so full of radiating love! So strong and penetrating was the gaze! Somebody stayed for a moment at an angle in front of me, between my friend and me. Tears came into my eyes. I sat as if I had died. But inside me warm life was pulsing.

At that moment she heard her friend, startled, call her name:

> 'Who is in this room? Turn on the lamp! Are you a medium? Turn on the light!'
>
> Somebody — yes, as certain as I am alive, this was our Redeemer who visited us for a moment, gave me from His warm, radiating human love, remained, gave my friend a strong perception that a Third One had been present.

The light was turned on, and the appearance faded. The woman saw the restless face, the fearful eyes of her friend. However, she herself felt weak and without strength. The friend brought her a drink of water.

The dramatic document ends:

> My good friend saw me to the door. 'Promise me that we never talk about this,' she said and looked rather frightened.
>
> It is a pleasure for me to personally bear witness to this occurrence. I am a very ordinary person. Through all these years and various trials this jubilant certainty has always been my staff and my shield,

even my solid ground. Through grace have I received proof that even today we have a living Master amongst us.

'As if a hand took my hand'

Report No. 53 is about a conversion meeting, obviously in the environment of the Free Church. From the document it follows that the person in question was in a conversion meeting. One does not learn whether the person in question was a man or a woman because the document contains only a signature and the name of a town.

> For a long time I had lived in misery of knowing that I was a sinner. I believed that God could not forgive such a great sinner like me. Others prayed for me, but I did not feel anything.
>
> But one day, a little later, something happened. I thought: 'How would it be if Jesus walked on Earth here and now and I could meet Him on the way? What would He then say to me? At that moment it was as if Somebody took my hand and led me, fast as lightning, on a long, long path until we came to Golgotha. Then the hand released me and I saw Jesus on the cross. He turned His head, looked at me and smiled. And His eyes radiated unspeakable love. Then I recognized it was I for whom He died, and my sins He bore. Then my heavy burden of sin fell off, and I felt indescribably happy.
>
> For almost a week I had this image in front of me; then it gradually faded until it was gone. But then I was a new human being. The old one had passed on; everything had been renewed. With all my heart I can join in the hymn 'When He saved me, took my sin unto Him, it was a miracle of limitless grace'.

A pierced hand on my head

A pastor in the Swedish Mission Society, born in 1917, wrote (Report No. 80):

I am taking the liberty to write and report of my experience, not that I have seen Jesus, but that I have sensed His presence and touch.

In October 1954 I got into a spiritual crisis or rather, a long-standing spiritual crisis came to a resolution, and in connection with this crisis peculiar spiritual experiences began for me. In December of 1955 I visited my district supervisor in order to speak with him about my experiences. After the conversation we prayed together. We knelt in front of his chair with about 1m (3') in between. When I had prayed for a while I was 'seized by the spirit'. At that, I do not determine what I shall say but the words are given to me. I was allowed to say: 'Thank You, Lord Jesus that you are here.' Then I heard as if an inner voice said to me: 'May it happen to you as you believe!' At that, I was allowed to sense that Jesus stood between us. Now I was permitted to say: 'And that You lay your pierced hands upon us!' Now I was privileged to feel on the top of my head a hand, and I felt that it had been pierced. He slowly leaned forward. My body was not relaxed because there was something I was not relieved of. (I was set free of it on 6 March 1956 [about a year and a half later].) I threw myself to the floor as He removed His hand. I stood up without assistance. That afterwards I was more in heaven than on Earth is obvious.

The blessing, healing hands of Jesus are so well known among themes of the New Testament that detailed comments seem to be superfluous. 'He laid His hands on them' as He blessed the children (Matt. 19:15). 'He laid His hands on each one and healed them all' (Luke 4:40). 'Then He touched their eyes' and healed the blind (Matthew 9, 29). 'Then He came to them and touched them' (Matt. 17:7). This last quote refers to the situation on the mountain of the transfiguration when the disciples had fallen on their faces and were 'much afraid'.

5. 'We got to know the difficulties of perception'

In a previous chapter (page 31) several words were quoted which we would like to repeat in order to take a closer look at them.

> As an artist I am very skeptical in regard to outer looks. We got to know the difficulties of perception and have discovered in the dilemma of the art of portraiture that how the outer looks shown are dependent on the one who sees them... [Report No. 82].

Perception means feeling or, in a wider sense, the ability to comprehend. The modern, scientifically acquired psychology could contribute a lot to what the quoted artist says about the uncertainties of perception.

This is true for anyone of us in daily life. What do I do when I want to describe what something looks like? Which comparisons do I try to use? How subjective is my perception when I say that somebody is beautiful, or when I indicate a colour, for instance, that the hair is chestnut brown? It is not certain that my friend who was present and saw the same thing would describe it in the same terms.

If what is said here is valid for perceptions in daily life, how much more would it apply to attempts to convey experiences, extraordinary to the individual in most cases, such as the appearance of a living Jesus.

In addition, everyone has different abilities to put into words and to describe what he or she experiences. The description of one person is more alive, that of another one less so. This becomes clear in the documents collected here.

But is it possible to explain significant differences through this? To explain how somebody could experience Jesus as wonderfully beautiful in contrast to another person seeing Him with less beautiful features would be easy to explain by means of the psychology of perception. But how can one explain that somebody sees Jesus in the shape of Thorvaldsen's Christ?

A Jesus who is like the Jesus of artists and poets ...

On a more scientific level, an attempt shall be made to provide commentary and explanations and, in a way, put up with all the uncertainties and misunderstandings involved in such an undertaking.

Before this happens there is good cause to list a number of striking coincidences between the reported experiences and the portraits of Jesus painted by artists and described by poets in order to widen the background. In this connection I will try, first of all, to remark only on similarities.

With regard to representations of Jesus by artists and to the submitted reports no comment is necessary. The material speaks for itself: several of the writers themselves refer to artists' pictures of Jesus.

The similarity with the Jesus of poets — or better, between the picture of Jesus by some poets and the presented material — is also easily proven.[10]

'You kind Jesus who stand ... beside Your Father,' Harriet Löwenhjelm writes. Nils Ferlin asks:

Can you hear Him,
As He comes as a Psalm,
So profound, as mysterious as a dream,
He wanders towards you
In the sultry heat of the day
And definitely does not
Want to harm you.

Many have read and loved this poem. In one of the reports, reproduced on page 56, the writer himself points to a poem by

Hjalmar Gullberg: 'Dreamed Visit'. In the poem 'Autumn Psalm' by Erik Axel Karlfeldt, Jesus comes during the stillness of dusk, lenient and kind:

> But I have heard the kind voice before,
> And it has followed me like the breath of the hazelnut shrub
> At the time when my heart went from door to door
> Like a beggar and every one was barred to me.

Karlfeldt also draws the picture of 'a blinding and fast vision' although the connection in the poem points to an evening experience:

> Your being came close to me during the splendour of the day
> Only like a blinding and fleeting vision,
> However, closer to the evening
> Under the wreath of thorny roses,
> And, closest, like a breath, a tone.

The similarity does not have to be overdone. In this case it appears more in the mood than in the content. But Karlfeldt, who got the inspiration for the poem during a stay in Assisi, shows Jesus as kind and gentle, just as Francis had experienced his Master.

Bo Setterlind in his poem 'The meeting of the Sinner with Christ' has drawn the picture of the 'kind Christ' who sits under a tree and plays and who answers the question of what He was doing: 'I am calling my sheep.'

We also meet a kind and gentle Jesus in the portraits of literature in prose, for instance in 'The Son of Man' by Emil Ludwig, and in 'The Man from Nazareth' by Schalom Asch.

The magnificent, beautiful Jesus

In the so-called Lentulus letter we have a famous description of the looks of Jesus. Lentulus is said to be the predecessor of Pontius Pilate and, therefore, a contemporary of Jesus:

In our time a man with great authority, named Jesus Christ, has appeared who is still alive. The people call him the prophet of truth, and his disciples call him the Son of God. He resurrects the dead and heals the sick.

He is a man of medium height and is well built. He has a venerable countenance which can rouse fear as well as love in those who encounter it.

His hair is of the same colour as that of ripe chestnuts, straight down to the ears, and it falls over his shoulders. It is parted in the middle, as is common among the folks living in Nazareth.

His forehead is even and very peaceful, and his face is free of spots and wrinkles and tends towards a slight red. His nose and his mouth are well-formed. His beard is full and unshaven and of the same colour as that of the hair, not long but parted to the chin.

His eyes are radiant and full of expression. He is terrible when he accuses, but friendly when he admonishes ... His figure is slender and upright. His hands and arms look handsome.

The Lentulus letter, which supposedly was addressed to the Senate, is a forgery when seen in the light of history. But it can also be looked at as something else, namely as the homage to Jesus by a poet.

How did the Lentulus letter, which probably has been written during the thirteenth century at the earliest, influence the image we have of Jesus? To find a just answer to this question is difficult. It is certain that the picture has had an impact, perhaps not at the least because the descriptive picture of Jesus is so attractive. The letter contains a description of Jesus which coincides with the imagination of many.

'He is the most handsome of all human beings.' This remarkable ending points to the way in which the text should actually be understood. In Psalm 45:2 we have a starting point for this 'painting'. The psalm can be interpreted as a prophecy of the coming king. Besides, in this psalm we can read: 'You are the most handsome among the sons of human beings; loveliness has been poured over your lips; this way we see that God has blessed you forever.'

In the Church of old there were no well-worn traditions about the outer looks of Jesus. It may be of interest that a few of the Church Fathers were of the opinion He appeared ugly or repelling. The Church Father Irenaeus, who died after the year 190, says that Jesus was hardly attractive, was unsightly, and frail. Origen (185–254), the most important theologian of the Eastern Church, writes that He was of small build and ugly. Cyril of Jerusalem (313–86), the patriarch of Jerusalem, goes farthest in this way; he is of the opinion that Jesus has been 'the ugliest of human beings'!

This odd tradition appears to be a counterpart to the line represented by the Lentulus letter. The tale of the beautiful Jesus is an interpretation of Psalm 45. The thought that Jesus was ugly likewise follows from an interpretation of the Bible. Isaiah 53:3 says: 'We hid, as it were, our faces from him.' And at another place: 'His looks were uncommonly disfigured.' Isaiah 53 is a prophecy of the suffering servant of the Lord and can be applied directly to Jesus.

As we have seen, of the two traditions which have lost every basis of the actual looks of Jesus the first one mentioned is, of course, the most appealing one. Meanwhile, one can cite other comments as explanation why the picture of the magnificent, kind Jesus has an impact. In poetry and in art, produced on the basis of the Christian faith, Jesus is usually described from the starting point that He was and is the Christ who has overcome suffering and death. Naturally one can also meet the picture of suffering, quite often in contemporary portrayals of Jesus. But above all, the victorious, glorified Christ has an inspiring effect: a living, risen Lord, above earthly limits and humiliations. It is easy to understand that the image of Jesus wears features of incomparable beauty.

'His eyes are full of expression and radiant' is written in the Lentulus letter. Does not the same thought repeatedly appear in the quoted documents, just dressed in varying expressions? In such a case the Lentulus letter would have had an influence on the image of Jesus; but this would be difficult to explain today.

What kind of effect, for instance, has Rembrandt's Jesus portrait had, emotionally and objectively, with regard to the image? The philosopher Karl Jaspers has tried to characterize it; and his words remind one of some descriptions our correspondents have tried to convey to us. Jaspers speaks of Rembrandt's Christ countenance 'as of unfathomable depth, full of strength and kindness, knowing and suffering'.

'Those who want to paint Christ have to live with Him.'

These words come from Fra Angelico (1387–1455). His image of Jesus is inwardly touching. He wanted to emphasize compassion and engaged himself for what he thought to be the right deed and the right ego of Jesus. The features of the Master are human and kind.

One could be critical of such a Jesus picture. When the words are taken from their context they still have to say something significant. The Jesus picture drawn receives its character as a genuine image from personal experience and engagement. Whoever goes about it in a critical and unengaged way would hardly be able to give us a picture of Jesus.

But does this not mean that the experience and its description must be coloured by the personal engagement? The answer to this is obviously 'Yes'. Artists who create spontaneously have confirmed this at times in peculiar ways. We have a Jesus of Africa painted as a black man; one as an Indian, with striking features of the Hindu art tradition, etc. In these cases a conscious, drastic interpretation can be seen, with the intent to form Jesus for the contemporaries and for those looking at the picture. On a more unconscious level evidently many Jesus experiences arise in the same way. If Jesus is to mean something to me then He must be so that I can understand Him.

In the psychologist's view with regard to the laws of perception, is it then so peculiar when the experience of Jesus has the character of that which we have read, heard or seen of Him? It is not peculiar, and the experience, therefore, does not have to be less genuine.

A few words of Johannes Jellinek are worth thinking about in this regard: 'The features of Jesus must not be cast into hard contours; and here it does not matter whether He wears a Jewish full beard or has a Roman smooth face. The figure of Jesus must not be fixed. For the Jesus figure of the Bible is Christ, the Word become flesh, in the faith of each believer.'[11]

In plain language it means: a certain measure of subjectivity is attached to every picture of Jesus. So it is not odd that this attitude appears also in documents relating experiences of Christ by human beings of today.

Jesus, Comforter and Helper

Whether Jesus had a full beard or not, nobody knows, not even the American professor one of the reporting persons speaks of.[12] On the very oldest pictures of the early Church Jesus is shown as a beardless youth. A more mature Christ figure with a bearded, vigorous face appears, in a historical sense, in later centuries.

When one really thinks about it, such details are quite uninteresting. Much more important is that the documents have a clear tendency to describe the good helper. Of the Jesus who looks around in anger very little can be found in the presented reports. Here the existential character of the reports shows itself anew and very distinctly: as a rule, it is about people who are in personal trouble. And in this situation Jesus appears as helper and comforter.

As shown above, the Jesus of artists and poets has, perhaps, played a role in this. But it is just as well possible to turn the course of thought around and say that the artists and poets have interpreted something important, a very genuine biblical theme. It is undisputed that in the New Testament He appears 'as a young man, firm in the devotion of His life' (Dag Hammersk-jöld), and not only as a Master who speaks 'like a tone of a soft violin', 'like the fresh coolness of the evening' (Nils Ferlin).

The reports in this book are to be considered as witnesses for Jesus, the comforter, the helper, the healer. In this way He also appears in the New Testament, according to His words, for instance in Matthew 11:28–30: 'Come to Me, all who have hardships and heavy burdens to bear. I will give you new forces of life. Take My yoke upon you and learn from My being: In Me, courage and humility of heart are combined. You shall find sources of new life-forces for your souls; for, My yoke is gentle, and my burden is light.'

On the whole, it is the Jesus of the Bible whom we meet in most of the reports: He who had promised to be forever with those who had found Him; He, the good shepherd; He who appears at the same time as the Risen One, alive and transfigured, full of strength and tenderness, with a gaze that sees through every-thing and yet is full of deep compassion.

6. Testimonies from the Past[13]

Confessions and reports of direct experiences of Christ are numerous, especially in medieval Christian mysticism, as is well known. Through Devotion to Christ, a movement started by Bernard of Clairvaux (1090–1153), the looking at, and contemplating of, the picture of the Crucified One, His countenance, His wounds, became more and more popular. The Jesus child, often depicted in the manger, also became the object of devout adoration. Above all, Jesus occurs in the medieval visions of the persons mentioned below. Many examples of this kind can be found among the church-related works of art of these times.

St Francis (1181/82 – 1226)

The turning point in the life of Francis was the remarkable experience in the partly ruined San Damiano chapel in the year 1208. At that time already Francis used to pray before the picture of the Crucified One in the chapel. Since his ambitions in regard to war-type achievements were made impossible he had years of searching behind him. The Byzantine crucifix he saw before him in the chapel depicted the bleeding Redeemer with a countenance showing peace and kindness. The Crucified One did not have closed eyelids but a downcast gaze, as of wanting to say, not 'I am suffering,' but 'Come to Me.' Francis had prayed that day: 'Great and venerable God and You, Lord Jesus, I am asking You, please let Your light shine into the darkness of my soul … Let me find You, O Lord, so that I may act only according to Your will.' The gaze of the Crucified One came alive, and in the stillness of the place Francis heard a voice: 'Francis, go out and raise My Church again; for you can see that it is threatened with total ruin.'

So tradition tells us. Without doubt, St Francis has spoken of this event to his followers. In his biographies it says, from this moment on, his heart was wounded and very sensitive as he thought of the Lord's suffering.[14] Some of his later biographies tried to lift the veil of the legend. Their writers are of the opinion that the words came out of the heart of Francis: 'but being in a trancelike condition he understood them as coming from outside and believed that they had been spoken by the figure on the cross'.[15] In any case, it is a decisive factor that Francis during his intensive looking at the Crucified One was able to have a vision of Him and hear Him speak.

True to his vision, Francis built the San Damiano Church, later on also the Portiuncula Chapel. It was here, on 24 February 1209, where Francis as the only worshipper heard the priest's words which so strongly revolutionized not only the Church but also the whole western world, words which lead to the breakthrough of the ideal of poverty and the idea of the Order of Begging Monks. 'When the priest addressed him, reading the words of Jesus, Francis became very excited. He saw not the priest any-more; it was Jesus, the Crucified One of San Damiano who spoke to him.'[16] These were the well-known words Jesus had spoken to send His disciples out into the world: 'Go out and proclaim the message: "The kingdom of heaven has come close." Heal the sick, awaken the dead, cleanse the lepers, drive out demons! You have received a free gift; now give freely. Do not acquire gold or silver or copper for your own pocket. You don't need a bag on your journey, nor a second coat, nor shoes or a staff. Whoever is active deserves to receive what he needs' (Matt. 10:7–10). Francis threw away his staff, tore off his sandals, also his belt, and became a begging preacher, 'the little poor one of God'.

The third Christ experience of Francis, on the Alvern Mountain on 14 September 1224, transformed him also physically. Jesus revealed Himself again as the Crucified One, as the man of suffering. Francis experienced again the grief of crucifixion on his body. He received the wounds of Christ as stigmatization. No historian is able to decide what really happened. According to Sabatier this story is available 'in a poetical, not reliable form'. But he himself adds: 'The opposite would be astonishing.' There is no reason to doubt the event. Francis had a vison early in the morning on the day of the celebration of the Raising of the Cross: he saw a seraph, wings spread out, soaring towards him. In the centre of the vision a cross could be seen.

In the popular Franciscan tradition, visions and revelations played a big part, already in earlier times. The well-known collection of legends 'The Wreath of Flowers of St Francis' by Fioretti contains a story how Christ appeared to brother Giovanni of La Vernia, one of the 'Sons' of St Francis.

Suso

In the cultural current originating with Meister Eckhart (1260–1328) the conscious vision was a highlight of religious life. The precondition was that the soul first was cleansed and freed from false images, from all those connected with the body, and then was opened to God who is born in the soul. It happens through the divine intellect that is in the soul. Of the students of Eckhart it is especially Suso (1295–1366) who uttered the thought of the human spirit 'crossing over' for the purpose of the union with God.

A different tradition originates with another student of Eckhart's, Tauler (1300–61). With him visions and visionary experiences played a minor part because the divine in the soul was considered to be a deep-rooted desire by the moral will. According to this, the union with God happens more often when the personal will is relinquished in quiet humility. Luther also was influenced by this mysticism. The divine vision appears rarely with Luther and with the tradition based on his teaching.

Suso had the distinct talent of a visionary. He was a Dominican; Dominic and other saints had appeared to him, and also Jesus – as a small child, as youth, but also as the Crucified One.

Suso had at least one vision of the Crucified One, similar to the great experience of Francis' stigmatization which apparently has had the effect of being a model. The Crucified One showed Himself below a picture of a seraph who had six wings. Two of them covered his head, two were on his feet and he used two to fly (cf. Isaiah 6:2) On the two lowest wings was written, 'Receive your suffering willingly', on the central ones, 'Bear your suffering with patience', and on the topmost ones, 'Learn to suffer, similar to Christ.' An illustration in a medieval manuscript shows the picture of Jesus on the cross, suspended above the ground, with wings above His head, above the arms and the hips—Jesus as crucified seraph.

St Birgitta (Bridget) of Sweden

In the great selection of Birgitta's revelations, the Christ visions constitute an important, but hardly predominant part, although the rules of the Order of the Saviour had been given to her 'from heaven through the mouth of Jesus Christ'. But often she saw others; she saw Mary, saints, contemporary persons. Above all, we know of her visions of Jesus during her childhood and on her deathbed. These were her first and last visions; but otherwise the revelation often was auditory, an experience of hearing, or of a sudden clarity of thought.

Birgitta saw Jesus as the Crucified One, saw Him as the small Jesus child, saw Him as the heavenly king or as judge. Several of her Jesus visions were a kind of repeated experience of scenes from the Gospels, were 'travels back in time'. She saw Jesus as He had lived, suffered and died for the world.

St Teresa of Avila

Teresa of Avila (1515–82) interpreted her own visions of Jesus partly as 'thoughts' or 'images', partly as 'intellectual' appearances. She saw the latter through an inner sight and heard through an inner hearing. The visions were part of the fourth stage of her inner prayer, the union with God, but were prepared during the first stage through intensive meditation of any event of the life of Jesus and His history of suffering, as if all this had happened while she prayed. At this stage Jesus did not appear as a concrete figure. 'I would not be able to imagine Christ as any kind of defined figure. I have read many descriptions of His outer looks and liked to look at pictures showing Him; but this did not help. When I thought of Him in my prayers it was as if a blind person or one in the dark is near to someone he knows. He understands and believes that the other is there; but he does not see him.'

The 'images' were not bodily visions but 'spiritual' ones: she never saw with her own eyes but with an inner sight. Such an image was the vision on 25 January 1568, when she saw the Saviour 'as one paints the Risen One, but of an incomparable beauty and a never seen majesty'. Here one could think of Birgitta's visions of the heavenly Christ; however, Teresa's were more connected to mysticism of light.

Johann Arndt

In the view of Luther's followers, a certain fear, not to say mistrust, of visions prevailed. Luther himself had experienced some appearances. Well known is that of the devil. His religious breakthrough, however, happened in connection with a Christ meditation he felt prompted to do by his friend Johann von Staupitz. Luther, in his desperation, received from him the advice: 'One must look at the man named Christ.' Luther also was in connection with German mysticism. As with Tauler and in the *Theologia deutsch*, its aims never were to have visions but to give up one's own will.

During the years of 1605 to 1609 Johann Arndt published four books on true Christianity. He understood Tauler and *Theologia deutsch* in the same way. Arndt emphasized that the human being could attain only 'in deep humility' the blessed eyes in order to 'behold Christ'. Arndt did not support the 'bride mysticism'. The bride, the soul, embraces the bridegroom, and in this embrace 'blessed conversations happen which no human ear has heard, no human eye has seen'; but only the humble ones will reach this stage. Arndt also speaks of the grace of light which the soul attains when the natural light is extinguished. Arndt then describes how the human being sees God in His splendour, God who is the most beautiful for the soul. But in his writings he never speaks of the seeing of Christ. However, he saw Jesus on his deathbed on the evening of 11 May 1621 ...

Swedenborg

Emanuel Swedenborg, the most eminent mystic of Sweden besides Birgitta, was deeply familiar with the western mystic tradition and also with the Jewish one. Already as a child he practised mystical exercises, as in imperceptible breathing or in striving for being lifted into higher realms while reading his evening prayer. He had his famous great vision of Christ on the second day of Easter, 6 April 1744. He himself has described what happened. He had read the Bible on the day before and had found that he did not have 'as strong a faith as was necessary'. He was challenged by doubt. Were the miracles possible which God had accomplished through Moses? In the end he had overcome his doubts and went to bed early. Half an hour later he heard a noise at the headboard. He took this for the leaving of the 'tempter'. It moved him deeply several times. Then he fell into deep sleep. A little later he was gripped by trembling from head to foot. Tremendous forces were in motion. It was as if many thunderstorms were unleashed. He prostrated himself. He thought he was awake, spoke as if he were awake. But it was not he who spoke; the words were put into his mouth. He prayed to Christ: 'O You almighty Christ, how can You condescend to come to such a big sinner — make me worthy of Your grace.' He lifted his hands, folded for prayer, prayed and felt a hand firmly embracing his hands. He continued his prayer, saying: 'You have promised forgiveness for all sins — You cannot do otherwise than to keep your promise.' 'At the same moment I was taken to His chest and saw Him face to face. It was a countenance with an expression so holy, and everything was so indescribable and kind so that I believed that He must have looked like that during His lifetime.'

The revelation follows the classical pattern of mysticism: the feeling of the lack of worthiness, the purification, the 'mystical joy', and finally the vision. This, however, provided no certainty but created an inner transformation in its wake. Through it a new inner human being grew forth and experienced his religious calling. Swedenborg experienced the certainty of his calling only a year later in London. 'Every day, several times, the Lord opened my bodily eyes so that I could speak with angels and spirits in a happy mood in the middle of the day.'

Sadhu Sundar Singh

The Christ vision of the Indian preacher Sadhu Sundar Singh (1889-1929) is extraordinarily noteworthy. It was a conversion vision with features similar to those experienced by Paul. At the time he was quite familiar with the Bible which he got to know in an American mission school. He found the words gripping: 'Come to Me, all who have hardships and heavy burdens to bear. I will give you new forces of life' (Matt. 11:28). And further: 'The Father showed His love for the world through this, that He offered up His only Son. From now on, no one shall perish who fills himself with His power; indeed, he shall win a share of the life that is beyond time' (John 3:6). But he was unable to give up

Hinduism. He became engrossed in its documents in order to refute Christ. But he found nothing that matched the words of Jesus he had read. In desperation he burned the Bible, the book promising peace and quiet but bringing him dissension and unrest. 'The religion of the West is wrong; we must destroy it,' he said to his father who asked him why he was doing such a foolish thing. It was 16 December 1904; he was 15 years old. He could not stop thinking about his assassination of the Bible. 'The memory that I had pursued Christ and torn up the Bible is a stinging thorn in my life.'

Meanwhile, this action had increased his restlessness. He decided to take his life. On this day he prayed: 'O God, show me the right way; otherwise I will take my life.' He prayed incessantly but received no answer. In the early morning he saw a bright light in his room. He thought the house was on fire, and opened the door; but there was no fire to be seen. He closed the door and continued to pray. Then he saw in a cloud of light a face radiant with love. First he thought it was Buddha or Krishna or another Indian deity. He wanted to fall down and pray to it. Then, to his great surprise, he heard the words in Hindi: 'How long will you pursue me? I have died for you. I have given my life for you' (cf. Acts 9:4). He was speechless and did not understand any of it. Then he became aware of the wounds of Jesus of Nazareth whom he had esteemed as a great man, who had died a long time ago in Palestine, whom he had hated later on, but who now was radiant with kindness and love. It became clear to him: 'Jesus Christ is not dead, He lives and this is He Himself.' He fell down, prayed, and soon his inner being was wholly transformed. When he got up Jesus had vanished.

Ever again, Sundar Singh came back to this: '*He showed Himself to me*. When He *revealed* Himself to me I saw His magnificence, and I knew that He was the living Christ.'

Our time is more open to experiences like this one and also for the interpretation Sadhu Sundar Singh has given it. The old, orthodox censors are gone. Many people got tired of the words and definitions. Behind these, one can sense a higher reality streaming in 'when the doors of perception have been purified' (William Blake). It is, however, remarkable that mystic experiences of Jesus now appear at a popular level. Popular piety has sources bubbling which have quite often been underestimated and misjudged by Churches and congregations.

7. What the Reporting Persons Themselves Find Significant

> Not even the fact that in my case nothing lasting came about can suggest the view that it was an illusion. Even if some psychologists should come to this conclusion after reading my communication it would not bother me at all. Everybody has the right and the duty to remain true to his experience. And through such faithfulness do not illusions change to realities, even to miracles which contain all the riches of eternity under the inadequate cloak of the moment? [From Report No. 90]

This consideration in regard to the character of religious experiences is essential and should be kept in mind by those who study them further. What is objective happens during the moment the vision or auditory happening is experienced, regardless of how the experience is being described scientifically or analysed psychologically. The experience can be of immense importance for the person who sees or hears Christ in His presence or experiences Him in another way. In this final chapter we shall venture the attempt to discuss the meaning of the experiences under different aspects.

For the most part, we shall let the documents themselves speak again. The attention shall be directed first to the way the reporting persons themselves have understood their experiences, in so far as they considered such questions. Was it 'something objective, something outside of myself?' Or just a dream? A voice inside me? And, in such a case, what was its meaning?

Assuming it was only a dream, is it not possible that it nevertheless has a special meaning, is a special message for me?

One informant writes of the 'extraordinary power of decisiveness' of his vision. Few go into such psychological considerations. But quite a number of them note that the experience has had an enormous significance for them personally.

It is easy to see that for the reporting persons the importance lay in their religious life. 'Therefore, God exists,' one person wrote. The essential significance of the experiences can be seen in the breakthrough of the religious dimension and in the strengthening of the life forces. Often with direct reference to the experience, all this leads further to the certainty, the confidence in life, to a life related to Christ.

'Something objective; something outside of myself'

Several contributions emphasized that the experience had the character of complete reality. Here is a text representative of this from Report No. 92:

> This event is neither fantasy nor imagination. I experienced it in a completely unexpected way. Also it is not a subjective vision but, as I have said before, it was something objective, outside of myself...

But also in cases when the informant proceeds from the fact that the experience had a different character than the sense perceptions of everyday life, the event can be of greatest significance — regardless of how it may have been described.

In Report No. 77 a man wrote how Jesus came to him during the night 'in a dream vision'. He told us what he saw and heard but emphasized again very clearly that the experience had the character of a dream.

> Immediately afterwards I woke up and asked myself what the experience could probably mean.

The question what significance the experience of having heard the voice of Jesus would have for him later on he answered himself:

This revelation has given me strength to endure the difficulties of my later life, and the words of Jesus to the head of the synagogue still stand before me.

The words in question are the same ones he had heard Jesus speak to him in his dream. 'Do not be afraid, only have trust' (Mark 5:36).

Experiences which provided certainty

In Report No. 9 the informant described his experience as a 'Golgotha vision' and told us how he saw Jesus had a gaze of 'unearthly love and of a kindness without limits' and turned towards him who experienced himself as one of the crowd who had brought Jesus to the cross. In the report one can read the comment:

Earlier in my life I did not believe in Jesus. But no one can take from me the certainty that He has risen and lives among us today and comes to individual human beings and is near us.

In Report No. 5 a woman told us how, after a period of great personal difficulties, she heard the voice of Jesus one morning. The main parts of the document were presented on page 17. The woman made the following comment:

The experience was a great help to me, thanks to the immense power lying in the words of Jesus. I know that *He* can penetrate the deepest darkness when we have faith and ask *Him*!

In the same report the woman told us of another vision. She worked as 'Samaritan' for children and thought she knew how great the need for care was in every congregation. In this work she experienced the inertia and slowness in the congregations and came across resistance everywhere. About five years earlier [in 1968] the following happened:

One day, when I had especially much to do I thought: 'From now on I won't be concerned any more with this work for the church. In order to have enough strength for this work I must give up trying to shake up the congregation. I have done my share. At this moment it was as if I received a strong electric shock and clearly heard the words: 'Let the children come to Me.' The voice was just as firm and at the same time tender and, I believe, the words had sounded like that when they were spoken for the first time.

The woman found this experience, as well as the one previously described, very significant for both her spiritual life and for her daily work.

Impressive in its simplicity is the remark added in Report No. 19:

There I saw Jesus stand at my side . . . I will never forget this vision. It was a realistic experience. Today I have peace and confidence in my life.

'So, then God exists'

Report No. 76 told us of an experience of light connected with the living God. Jesus was not mentioned in this context. The experience had decisive religious consequences.

Now I am 54 years old, and the event I want to talk about happened when I was between 35 and 40. Perhaps I should mention that my philosophy of life was purely atheistic at the time and had been that since my sixteenth year. The following happened.

It was an evening like any other. Around 10 o'clock I was preparing to go to bed. (I had not taken any tablets nor had I drunk alcohol.) I sat on the edge of the bed, felt a little tired, worn out, and 'empty', as the saying goes. Then, quite suddenly, it happened. I felt (one can hardly say 'saw' since it was not a physiologically imparted seeing), I felt a light, an intense, almost blindingly intense, light. I was filled with amazement, intense joy, happiness, awe. It was as if I had got into contact with something very, very holy, so majestic that I almost wanted to hide my face in my hands. The thought I had was: 'So, then God exists!' It is difficult to say how long the experience lasted, but it was so intense that in the end it was almost not to be borne. I thought I would perish if it took any longer.

The same report continued:

Any words become so poor and inadequate when I describe what happened. After this experience I have read many a book from which I gathered that I probably have had a so-called 'mystical experience'. It has, as I have said, also changed my views on life.

Proof that even today we still have a living Master among us

Some documents show quite dramatically how a human being who has experienced the living Christ has reached such a certainty through this that nothing can take that away from him.

Here we recall how in Report No. 63 a nurse told us that soon after her exam she had a dispute with a school friend about her faith in God. The friend attacked her: could she say anything that proved or confirmed her statements? Tired, she reclined in her chair. Then Jesus came — so her experience — and stayed for a few seconds between her and her friend who experienced that something extraordinary was happening and was frightened. The young nurse saw Jesus, remembered His eyes and His firm gaze full of love.

After 30 years the experience is still as significant for her as it was then. It had given her a 'jubilant certainty'. She 'had received proof that even today we still have a living Master among us'.

'The cross in the sky: revelation for strengthening the faith'

We bring the following document in its entirety. Most likely commentaries are unnecessary. Even this heading is from the man who is the author of Report No. 6. His age or profession were not mentioned. The letter is from a town in central Sweden.

I had parents who were strong in their faith. Often they included me in their prayers. For ten years I myself prayed that God may show me a sign as proof of His existence so that I would not fall into doubt.

The preacher in my home town who liked to draw once gave me one of his drawings entitled 'Christ on Golgotha' with the caption 'With this sign you will be victorious'. I did not think much about it until in 1950 I experienced an appearance I will never forget.

We had gathered for a prayer meeting in the home of my brother. While we prayed, God in His spirit came so near to us that it seemed the gate of heaven had opened. Later when we went outside a friend and I stood in conversation when suddenly the horizon became bright and out of this shining a cross appeared, radiant as gold. This phenomenon lasted about a minute, then dissolved and disappeared.

My friend had not noticed anything and I was so astonished that I never got to tell what I had seen.

After this remarkable experience I never needed to be in doubt that God exists. And I believe that this serious message was not meant for me alone but also for many people in our world who are entangled in doubt and depression.

I would like to add that I had never experienced any illusions that would have had an effect on my mental balance. And therefore I look at this as a pure miracle and greeting from a world which none of us normally sees.

The last remark of the writer shows that he is apparently of the opinion that his experience has the characteristics of reality, despite the fact that he is aware of the possibility of illusions.

'The strength of the vision and the enormous decisiveness'

Report No. 60 — partly reproduced on page 16 — told us how Jesus, as a figure of light during the dark of night, came to a 22-year-old man who was in bed, sick and depressed. The young student experienced the countenance of Jesus as an admonition: 'Seek Me'. Immediately after this it said:

The strength of the vision, the identity with Christ, has shown itself by the enormous decisiveness it has had on my life which afterwards was governed by Christ, both in theory and in practice. Don't conclude from this that I would be a saint—far from it! But what I want to say is: although I would be able to understand the vision and its prerequisite, none of this is of importance or it simply stands beside the fact that it was Christ.

In this context it may be noted as an objective fact that the informant who is now in retirement had been fond of being active as a lay preacher. He also had been a teacher of religion.

'The confidence is indescribable'

A man who has a white-collar job wrote and told us of an experience of light that gave him complete certainty regarding the existence of God, and confidence in his Christian life (Report No. 67).

Such an experience leaves strong traces, but not in outer life which stayed unchanged ... On the other hand, the faith stands like a rock. After all, I myself have experienced all this with my own senses. The confidence is indescribable. Whatever will happen, nothing can hurt seriously. I consider death as a gate one passes through towards truth, towards light, towards freedom and joy.

In report No. 100 (compare page 20) a Norwegian woman said she felt left alone by God on the evening before a serious operation. A vision of Jesus gave her confidence again. She experienced Christ standing at her bed saying, 'I am the chief surgeon.' The woman wrote that on that evening she would have lost her faith otherwise. Now she lives from what she has experienced. She tries to testify to this. Among other things she had ordered an article about faith healing to be translated from the English. 'I have sent it to a thousand well-known persons of our Church. It is as if an irresistible urge moves me to do a good work in order to promote the kingdom of God.'

Perhaps it was only after the Christ vision that I dared to count myself in earnest as a Christian. I believe that through this I have understood the second article of the creed. [Report No. 98]

In this way a woman concludes her report of a Christ experience. She had felt the touch of the hand of Jesus and grasped – without having heard human words – the deepest mystery of the cross when she saw that the shadow of the wooden cross in the window frame actually was the mirror image of an infinite cross outside that reached up to the clouds of the sky. And this experience gave her infinite peace, joy and security.

'I needed this in order not to doubt God's love'

Why? Why exactly me? Such questions were formulated directly or indirectly in several documents.

An answer which seems to be representative for many can be found in report No. 92:

Through such an event the thought could arise that one is more privileged than others. But it is *not* so. I needed this experience in order not to doubt God's love.

He who wrote these words tells first of personal difficulties he had when reading the story of Job; he began to doubt God. The document shows the following remarkable conclusion:

It is blessed to see and to believe; but it is more blessed not to see and believe anyway. The greatest of all probably is to be allowed to believe in Jesus as the Son of God, in the forgiveness of sins and in eternal life.

This confession was formulated by a businessman.

An exception: 'I do not attribute any significance to it'

Almost all who wrote attach very great significance to their experiences. But there are a few exceptions. One report speaks of a Christ vision similar to the Christ figure by Thorvaldsen. The writer says:

> I don't attribute any religious significance to all this but explain it in the same way a cross can come about on the moon through a certain configuration of light rays.

In this case it is not clear from the description whether the experience had been preceded by an intense engagement.

The precious secret

The experience was often characterized as a precious secret. Wäino Aaltonen who had met Christ in a dream and had learned to see colours with new eyes reported only much later about this in his book 'What Christ taught me'. 'I kept this to myself but told my father about it shortly before his death.' Later on he also told his mother about it because she feared that her son could become arrogant through winning the three first prizes in the competition for the Alexis-Kivi statue.

The shyness to communicate was striking in many reports. Often the writers stressed that they did not wish to have their names published.

> The experience of Jesus I had is so great and holy for me that I told of it only to a few of my best friends. [Report No. 43]

> And to this hour I divulged [this secret] neither to my wife nor to anyone else. But when I heard about the enquiry then after some time I felt obliged to participate. I did so, however, not to give a personal testimony but to serve the theological science and with it indirectly the Christian, spiritual life; under the condition that my contribution fits the context. [Report No. 90]

> I did not tell of this experience to many people, partly because one is concerned about such an experience—one does not want to become personally exposed—and partly because there are no adequate

words to describe what I have experienced. [Report No. 76, compare page 82]

The document described an experience of intensive light, which the informant himself called a 'so-called mystical experience'.

'A risk that others could take me for an eccentric'

'I felt no need and have had no occasion to share my experiences with someone else.' So wrote a sales agent (Report No. 67) who eleven years earlier had written down a detailed description of an experience of intensive light and of God (dated 20 February 1962). He thought it to be of mystical character.

Until now I have felt it to be an extraordinary experience for myself . . . Not even my family has learned of it.

He indicated two reasons why he has avoided publicity: one was quite personal; the other one had to do with the cultural situation in which we live and with religious prudishness that, in his opinion, prevails.

The publication of such an experience would not only mean the risk that I might be seen as wanting to be important, to gain honour, which would not be due to me. Others could take me for an eccentric. And through this, the message of the experience as proof for the reality of the other world would be diminished and thwarted. As far as I know, it is a great prejudice that Christians are expected to be different or that Christianity is seen as denying life, as being characterized by dark, difficult, gloomy demands. Christianity and material life are not in contrast with each other. On the other hand, life in the material world is unable to be really complete without the Christian insight.

8. Religious-psychological Comments

Attempts to explain psychologically the origin of the visions and auditions are of little importance

The statement of this title may, first of all, seem surprising. Nevertheless, so it is.

Only a small number of those reporting had touched on the psychological side of the experiences themselves. The quotation at the beginning of this report (page 78, Report No. 90) says that the informant was unconcerned about the interpretation by psychologists. 'Each person has the right and the duty to remain true to his or her experience.' Another example can be taken from Report No. 60 (quoted on page 16). The person, now an elementary school teacher in retirement, saw Christ come out of the dark when he was a young student. He said he had always been very interested in psychology and in the science of education. He wrote that he 'could theoretically understand the origin of the vision', but that the 'impact on his life' had been decisive. Especially it was the power of Jesus' eyes, that remained in his memory. He did not go into psychological questions in greater detail and, strictly speaking, found them unimportant.

One could dare to claim — and the material tends in this direction — that not the question how the visions and auditory experiences came about was important to these people but what consequences arose for them at the moment of the experience and afterwards.

Is Christ really present?

Hjalmar Sundén, professor for the psychology of religion, in his comprehensive book 'The Religion and the Roles' (in connection with a description of an auditory experience of Christ at the Front in France, 1917, by the Englishman Charles E. Raven) has asked the question about the presence of Christ. Since that time, and for a long time, this soldier has had the intense feeling of Christ on his side. 'I was never alone and never—except for a few moments—gripped with terror.'

Sundén adds to this in his writing—and one cannot disregard the answer:

> Psychology is unable to answer decisively a question of the kind: 'Is Christ really present?' What it can say is only this: each experience of Christ must have the prerequisite of a specific constellation of consciousness, that is, the individual must have acquired the Christian tradition in such a way that he or she can anticipate the appearance of Christ through any identification. Psychologists can *never deny* that the factor causing the course [of the experience] is of a *nature unknown to us*, for instance, really Christ ... But this does not change anything in the sequence of thoughts in psychology: without a constellation of consciousness which results in the interpretation 'Christ' there cannot be any human experience of Christ.

It is not the origin of the vision, the auditory experience, that is significant, as far as it is about a perception in general or one parallel to a daily occurrence, for instance, when I see or hear another person speaking when coming into the room. It keeps its specific, particular value through the effect caused by it—or, say, its message—even if the experience of the presence of Christ has a different character, for instance, than that of a hallucination.

In explanation, an example from a published report about the origin of the Inner-European Mission (IM) is reproduced here.

Britta Holmström's auditory experiences

When the Lord approached the heart of one of His human children with His arousing ardour—it was on the morning of 1 October 1938—then the word of the Lord sounded through this human being:

'A new mission shall begin—a new mission shall be started.' The words sounded over and over. My lips, however, refused to make them my own. It was just too much for me. I remained silent.

So the Lord appeared more and more powerfully to His child, and the commandment continued.

This quote is from the history of the origin of IM, the great relief organization first called 'Internal European Mission', later 'Individual Human Aid'.[17]

A young woman with a university education heard this commanding voice. She hesitated, but soon obeyed and took on the seemingly impossible task of engaging large sections of the population of our country for a relief action outside of Sweden.

The psychological background is easy to describe. Britta Holmström herself has summarized it in the same document: 'Earlier the heart of this human being was bursting with thoughts of our European brothers and of the untold misery which threatened to roll a war and violence across all of us.' The first goal of action stood clearly before her eyes: 'When in September, 1938, the clouds of war began to mount in earnest and in October the nightmare of violence attacked the Czech people, it became clear as lightning to her: "The mission will start here! Prague will be our first point of contact".'

A young university graduate who suffered intensely from the pressure of tyranny and evil in the world felt charged with an astonishing energy for action. In this case the decisiveness of the auditory experience could be described. Where did it come from? Hjalmar Sundén notes that in this case it is possible to state this, thanks to the description of the previous day given by the husband: days of devotion and of Bible studies.[18]

The deciding factor, however, is not that Britta Holmström heard a voice but its interpretation. What does it matter whether this was, in the psychological sense, a speech which formed in her subconscious? But what matters is the interpretation, the meaning. Or more distinct and properly expressed: interpretation in connection with an action of obedience.

The psychological background is, therefore, a violent, inner struggle for clarity, paired with a hot will to do something for the suffering fellow human beings. The struggle continued from the moment of the auditory experience until an interpretation and personal comment follow.

From a religious-psychological standpoint, the description which follows is especially interesting because the moment of interpretive structuring of the experience is so obvious. The interpretation in connection with the obedience happened after a struggle when the voice was temporarily interpreted as something else, a fantasy.

The situation was as follows. During the spring of 1948 IM had received the offer to take over the home for children, named 'Beach', in Reftele, from a Protestant nursing organization. A detailed quotation is of interest here. Folke Holmström described the following:

> It was an advantageous offer because the rooms were available free of charge, on condition that certain renovations were made. As chairperson Britta Holmström would have to visit the property in haste, at 9 a.m. on 9 April, the same day she would have to present the offer at 5 p.m. to the yearly congress of IM in Jönköping. Two days before, when my wife came home she was very tired. The children were sick, the youngest one, Erland, was developing pneumonia with a high fever (40°C). Under these circumstances the mother thought it to be impossible for her to take the fast evening train on 8 April. Since the children showed no improvement she finally went to bed late without a thought of reaching the last nightly train.
>
> A few minutes before 3 a.m. she woke up because Someone was standing beside her bed saying: 'Get up and travel! I will take over your home.' At the same moment she remembered that there was a slower train leaving at 3:27, which would still make it possible to reach the home for children on time. She went to the bed of her child and saw that he was still breathing heavily. She said to herself: 'It would be madness to trouble about the German children in danger of catching tuberculosis when my own child has pneumonia.' At that

moment she heard the unyielding voice again: 'Obey! I will bear responsibility for your home.' She woke her husband, informed him of what had happened; he agreed and ordered a taxi. She reached the train and arrived in the morning at the agreed time for the inspection of the house. All this made it possible that subsequently IM was able to take over the home for children.

The document is of great interest because it shows clearly that, at first, doubts about the correctness of the voice appeared. It was an intellectually trained woman who knew a lot about psychology and heard a voice. From this point of view, decisive is not the auditory experience but the obedience to it. *Just a vision or hearing a voice does not mean that the experience is a religious one.*

From a provocative document

Report No. 64 did not bring a detailed description of a vision or auditory experience. For the discussion in this chapter it is nevertheless of great interest to quote this report. The informant wrote that he had received a 'baptism in the Holy Spirit' during the winter of 1950/1, and on the basis of this experience he made a remark of great psychological and religious importance.

First he admitted his hesitation. He did not have much interest in telling what he had seen and heard. 'Only a small number of people are in such a spiritual situation that it is worth it and makes sense to present and analyse such experiences in detail.' The person in question fears misunderstandings. It is important to him to prevent these: he speaks of the greatest experiences of his life, of the most important ones, because they have to do, for the most part, with personal guidance.

According to his words, it is important to dissociate the interpretation not only from small-time psychology but also from parapsychological speculation.

Here I would like to insert that I do not mean any form of extra-sensory perception (ESP). There is a widely held interest in parapsychological cases which, by themselves, can be very interesting but can lead onto sidetracks.

What would be the characteristics of extraordinary religious experiences so that they could be classified as such? Our informant had the following answer:

> Perhaps one can distinguish these experiences from others by saying that here it is a question of a spiritual background, that they are connected with a spiritual faith, with a spiritual struggle, and that they are aimed at spiritual development and awakening.

Without going into his own personal experiences the writer stressed that they came 'after a spiritual struggle, a struggle for prayer which was connected with big temptations'. From the report we bring a longer quote here which starts with a short description of the kind of experiences he has had:

> Most of the visions I have had came to me during sleep, a smaller number while I was awake. I also have had an 'out-of-body experience'.
>
> Contrary to what one gets to hear now and then, I have valued the dream revelations and those during the day as completely equivalent. It even happened that I have seen such a revelation during sleep, followed by a later continuation when I was awake.
>
> Quite contrary to what is often said, I am not prepared to agree that the revelations and visions which appear in our time are supposed to be of lesser quality or reliability than those reported in the Bible. I also don't believe that one could prove such an assertion by means of consulting the Bible. Those who have tried this have, in my opinion, made an error in logic.
>
> However, what matters are the interpretations of what the persons have seen or heard. Here the difficulties begin. When I first had such experiences I was of the opinion that it was easy to interpret them, at least for the person having received them. Meanwhile I had not understood that in this way the revelations could become a substitute for faith. Now I know that visions are an aid to faith. Not all of them are clear; but they are sufficient. The secular human being wants to have revelations, so he or she does *not have to believe*. The

spiritual human being needs revelations once in a while in order *to be able to believe.*

The statements made in this document are extraordinarily interesting. Later on we will have occasion to discuss them and come to certain conclusions in comparison with the material previously presented.

The border between the healthy and the unhealthy-pathological in religious experiences

A vision or auditory experience can be an unusual expression of a developed spiritual life. An unusual religious experience can take on a great meaning, partly in a subjective way for the person experiencing it, as a basis for confidence, even as a precious experience of enormous decisiveness, and partly in an objective way through what it sets in motion. Hjalmar Sundén has very well summarized this aspect by pointing to the auditory experience of Britta Holmström: 'A new mission shall begin.' Sundén writes: 'I could quote many cases which correspond to what happened to Mrs Britta Holmström in Lund when she received the impulse to found a new mission. Together with her husband she lent 500 kronas, and after a few years values of 50 million kronas were supplied to needy human beings.'

The genuine vision or auditory experience is a precious, personal experience and is not made public without hesitation. Whoever experiences the extraordinary looks back astonished and thankful—astonished that just he or she, of all people, was allowed to meet such a great event. This circumstance explains why the occurrence of such experiences has been considered isolated. To the contrary, our reports show that visions and auditory experiences and the intensive experience of the presence of Christ generally happen more often than the majority of psychologists of religion imagine. The initiators probably would have received a much larger number of reports had the experiences not been considered to be so precious by many that they did not wish to come forward. Fear of being misunderstood and the religious prudery quite prevalent in our country can also have contributed to this. In any case, one can suppose that further material will be collected.

In many cases the genuine vision or auditory experience is a unique event. In any case, it is not an everyday experience. It fills the man or woman to whom it happens with astonishment and awe. The memory of it is sacred. The very thought of wanting to have new experiences is far from their mind.

The last-mentioned point of view at least is a criterion of dissociation from the unhealthy-pathological. In Report No. 64, just mentioned, this dissociation is built in through several statements pointing in several directions. The religiously unhealthy, pathological mind is able to indulge in 'revelations' and endeavours to receive ever new ones. The extraordinary experience — repeated often if possible — is considered, in the worst case, a criterion of a deeper spiritual life. Inclinations in this direction among religious extremist groups probably have heightened the fear of others to speak at all of religious experiences. This is understandable — one could add — since the border between the healthy and the pathological is transitional. Who wants to deny that St Birgitta was a genuine seer? And yet many of her revelations were fierce attacks in the form of supposed revelations, as proven by Sven Stolpes ('Birgitta in Sweden', 1973, e.g. page 194).

The genuine vision or auditory experience appears as the answer to a lengthy — or as an exception, to a short, but deeply shattering — spiritual struggle. But in this struggle no 'sign' of the kind meant here is asked for. The genuine vision or auditory experience comes as a surprise, suddenly and deeply moving. Usually the interpretation is clear immediately. The decisive point is the address and the commandment and what is being said or given — consolation, satisfaction, etc.

On the other hand, if the religious life is more characterized by repeated 'revelations' the interest is directed easily towards those. In spite of the usual term *revelation*, much will then become unclear and dark. Incidentally, it could perhaps be remarked that such difficult cases can also be found in many documents that have become part of the history of the religions and of the Church. The border between healthy and unhealthy is not always easily drawn, in psychic life as well as in the religious one.

One does not get visions from hysteria. A striking result of our investigation should be that those who came to the unusual religious experiences are healthy men and women and do not have to be somehow eccentric or strange human beings. This conclusion is fundamental and should impress itself deeply into the general consciousness.

The value of the genuine vision or auditory experience consists of the tangible experience of news having a clear religious content, occasionally also a distinctly ethical character. The certainty and conviction resulting from it and not the unusual phenomenon as such are what is decisive from the religious-ethical point of view. This must be kept in mind, even when the unusual experience by itself can appear as being very valuable. That is why the author of the Report No. 64, mentioned above, is right when he does not want to give priority to the extraordinary experience over others, in principle not even over a dream. By the way, in the Bible the religious importance of a dream can be found often.

Comparisons with the biblical stories

When we turn our attention to the descriptions how Jesus revealed Himself to His disciples after the resurrection from death then we notice in the material of the New Testament a clear tendency to emphasize the objectivity of the event, in the sense that it is not about stories of experiences one or more disciples have had. In the New Testament the character of the descriptions of the resurrection, like the description of the 'empty grave', has been a theme for virtually endless discussions among theologians and historians. The way in which the descriptions actually exist does not allow one to overlook that they differ from the ones mentioned above.

Among others, the differences are as follows.

In the New Testament, in some cases, Jesus showed Himself to several persons at the same time, as well as to all apostles, as at one occasion to five hundred persons, according to a report by Paul (1 Cor. 15).

Jesus, described in the New Testament as the Risen One, appears, to be sure, somehow transfigured in His form but is able to break bread with His disciples (Luke 24:30, in Emmaus) and to eat with them ('fried fish and honeycomb', Luke 24:42-3).

The risen Jesus walks together with His disciples, according to the stories of the Gospels.

The visions outlined in this book have a character different from those about the risen Jesus in the New Testament. The people reporting are intensively conscious of Jesus' presence. It is really Jesus Christ who is with them — they are convinced of this. But the presence has a different character: as to time, it is a question of seconds or minutes, and the image of Jesus is the image of a human being and yet something different. *The informants are aware they have had a vision of Jesus. Their descriptions differ from those of the New Testament.*

There is another essential difference, perhaps not noticed on first encountering it. In the New Testament as well as in the documents here reproduced, Jesus comes suddenly, completely unexpected. In considering the last-mentioned word 'unexpected', a difference rather than a coincidence emerges. The disciples do not expect at all that Jesus will go on showing Himself to them. They mourn His death. The people who have Christ visions in our time have heard of a living Christ since their childhood. Most of them have a strong faith in His strength and ability to help them.

In conclusion, one could say: *Today the visions of Christ have the prerequisite of faith in the resurrection, as instilled by the New Testament. The descriptions of the New Testament are, in one respect, something like models for every experience of a living, present Christ in later times. But those models are described more like visions, even in the New Testament itself.* That Jesus showed Himself as being alive, that He ate with the disciples, etc. is being described as a fact come true — as a surprising and, for the disciples, overwhelming fact.

However, it is this conviction, then and now, that Christ is alive — and here the agreement appears again. *In the end, this conviction is the prerequisite for visions of Christ.* Is it really the same Jesus Christ who appears anew but, then as now, just as surprisingly and overwhelmingly?

On this question one can comment — either in faith or in doubt.

Notes

1. Rudolf Steiner, *The Gospel of Luke* (1909), Lecture 7; *The Gospel of John in Relation to the Three Other Gospels, especially to the Gospel of Luke* (1909), Lecture 10; and other works.
2. Rudolf Steiner, *The Reappearance of Christ in the Etheric,* a collection of lectures (1910 to 1917) on the second coming of Christ, introduced by Stephen Usher.
3. 'The Appearance of Christ in the Etheric', lecture of 25 January 1910, GA 118, pp. 22-4.
4. 'The Inner Aspect of the Social Question', lecture of 11 February 1919, GA 193, pp. 60 f.
5. Remark of the translator into German: In this chapter the knowledge of customary Swedish conditions, Church customs and geographical places is taken for granted. The translation follows the book word for word. Knowledge of circumstances, perhaps not known to the reader, is, however, not essential for understanding the theme of this book.
6. Authorized Version of King James.
7. Free rendering.
8. As written in this book.
9. Ibid.
10. In Swedish poetry one can often meet the *kind Jesus*. In my book 'Who are you, Jesus?' I have given characteristic examples in the chapter 'Jesus—kind or coarse?'
11. 'Jesus figures in the Bible'. Essay in the Swedish magazine 'Christian Positions of Studies', 1967.
12. See page 46.
13. Remarks of the translator into the German: This chapter of the German edition [and, therefore, also of the English one] is a shortened selection of notes Berndt Gustafsson excerpted from well-known sources of the older Christian mysticism. The 'testimonies' are connected with the following names: St Francis, Suso, Birgitta (Bridget), Teresa of Avila, Johann Arndt, Swedenborg,

Sadhu Sundar Singh. These portrayals are not systematic but rather have the character of excerpts of the literature. One may assume that they have been introduced rather to point out to some modern readers the ways of the older mysticism of the 'Saints' than in order to compare them with the documents of our time. These are distinguished from those in that they just do not originate from exceptional individuals. To this, Gustafsson draws our attention with impressive words at the end of this chapter. The text has been shortened especially with regard to the revelations of Birgitta, which presumably were presented in more detail in view of the Swedish readers.

14. Paul Sabatier.
15. Ernest Raymond.
16. Paul Sabatier.
17. The document can be found in its entirety in the book by Folke Holmström 'Compassion with humanity, a path out of the crisis of the present?' (1957).
18. F. Holmström, pp. 28–31.